THE NEW MORTGAGE INVESTMENT ADVISOR

Structuring Your Mortgage to Work as A Financial Planning Tool

Peter D. Mitchell
James D. Pidd, II

ANDERSON-NOBLE PUBLISHING, LLC
LONG BEACH, CALIFORNIA

Copyright © MMVII by Peter D. Mitchell and James D. Pidd, II.

All Rights reserved. No part of this publication may be reproduced or transmitted in any form or by any means electronic or mechanical, including photocopy, recording, or any information storage and retrieval system now know or to be invented, without permission in writing from the publisher, except by a reviewer who wishes to quote brief passages in connection with a review written for inclusion in a magazine, newspaper, or broadcast. Published by Anderson – Noble Publishing, LLC, 6285 East Spring Street, Suite 387, Long Beach, California, 90808-4000. First edition.

Visit our Web site at **www.NewMortgageInvestmentAdvisor.com** or **www.CMIADesignation.com** for more information on the subjects covered in this book.

Although the authors and publisher have made every effort to ensure the accuracy and completeness of information contained in this book, we assume no responsibility for errors, inaccuracies, omissions, or any inconsistency herein. The ideas and concepts described in this book may not be applicable for all people. Laws, taxes, mortgage programs, insurance products and investment products are in a constant state of flux. Due to this, some parts of this book may be out of date even at the time of publication. The authors, publishers, & Capital Republic Financial Group, Inc., assume no responsibility for actions taken by readers based on the advice from this book. Seek the advice from a competent professional before implementing any these concepts.

ISBN 978-0-9754819-5-0 Hardback
ISBN 978-0-9754819-7-4 Paperback

Library of Congress Control Number: 2007928512

We would like to thank the many publishers and individuals who granted us permission to reprint the cited material. All copyrighted material was used by permission.

Published in the United States of America by
Anderson – Noble Publishing, LLC
6285 East Spring Street, Suite 387
Long Beach, Ca 90808-4000

ATTENTION LENDERS, BROKERS, CORPORATIONS, UNIVERSITIES, COLLEGES, AND PROFESSIONAL ORGANIZATIONS: Quantity discounts are available on bulk purchases of this book for educational, gift purposes, promotional, or as premiums for increasing magazine subscriptions or renewals. Special books or book excerpts can be created to fit specific needs. Write to Director of Special Projects, Anderson – Noble Publishing, LLC, 6285 East Spring Street Suite 387, Long Beach, California, 90808-4000, for information on discounts and terms. For faster service, email dsp@CapitalRepublic.com. You can also call (800) 990-2734.

Peter D. Mitchell would like to dedicate this book to...

    My wife Jami. You are the one that makes my life fun. I have always wondered what you see in me, but I have never questioned what I see in you. I look forward to what tomorrow brings so long as you are by my side.

    My mother and father, my desire is to make you proud.

    My mother-in-law, you are unforgettable!

    The Almighty.

James D. Pidd, II would like to dedicate this book to...

    My wife Karen and my children Timothy and Gwendolyn. You are the reasons made flesh for all my hard work.

    My mother Denise, my first and best financial advisor, who taught me the virtues of frugality, discipline, and hard work.

    My God- Soli Deo Gloria

Table of Contents

	Page

Chapter 1 7
The Financial Elephant in the Room

Chapter 2 19
The Traditional Mortgage: Why we do what we do

Chapter 3 33
Building a Better Mousetrap

Chapter 4 65
Maximizing Cash Flow

Chapter 5 89
Maximizing Cash Flow, Minimizing Risk

Chapter 6 109
Buying a New Home
    Examples 118

Chapter 7 125
Where to Put the Extra Money
    Examples 162

Bonus: Equity Wealth Seminar Tickets 171

Appendix I- CMIA Designation 173

Appendix II- Glossary of Mortgage Terms 177

About the Authors 191

Chapter 1
The Financial Elephant in the Room

Chapter 1
The Financial Elephant in the Room

A multitude of Americans are at the brink of a crisis. Newspapers across the nation, however, are largely silent in regards to it. Headlines surround us regarding rising fuel prices, global warming, terrorism, and a whole host of other issues. However, while many Americans are alarmed by all of the political issues of the day, they are unaware of a far more threatening, far more personal crisis that is looming just ahead. The threat is that of retirement and American's ability to afford living through their golden years.

The purpose of this book is not to alarm and use scare tactics to give Americans yet another issue to worry about. Rather, it is to help Americans realize that while all of the issues facing our communities, our nation, and the world are significant, none of them can be solved, let alone even seriously considered, if our own financial houses are not in order. A simple example will best illustrate the point.

Envision whatever political, social, or religious issue you are most connected with. For some it may be helping reduce the air pollution in their community. For others it may be donating to help starving children. Regardless of what issue (or issues) you have picked, for most of us there will always be a barrier that separates our desire to help and our ability to help. That barrier is that we have finite resources, both in regards to time and money. All of these issues you have envisioned are certainly worthy. All of them deserve our attention. Further, these are the issues that most motivate us. Yet, for most Americans, these issues will never be seriously attended to because we have failed to adequately plan for our individual futures, let alone a favorite charity or cause.

While local, national, or international events are stimulating to some, for many of us our own individual well-being is a significant enough issue to deal with. Will we be able to take the grandkids out to dinner when they visit? Will we be able to take vacations once the daily grind of going to work is behind us? These questions and thousands more like them resonate with the hearts and minds of most of us.

Whether we are motivated by issues extrinsic to us as individuals or simply want to focus on ourselves, the ultimate irony is that while we worry and fret over issues that are largely out of our hands as individuals, we ignore a huge issue that we as individuals can take control of. Again, the issue is that of proper financial planning and how it relates to proper mortgages for homeowners.

Leaving behind the pitiable picture of the unprepared retiree, the focus of this book is four-fold:

Goal #1- To make people aware of the learned habits that hinder their endeavors to get their financial houses in order

Goal #2- To motivate people to take a proactive role in getting their financial houses in order, especially in regards to retirement

Goal #3- To help people establish clear financial goals, especially in regards to retirement

Goal #4- To provide people with information regarding new methods in the mortgage industry that can lead to the creation of tremendous personal wealth

With these goals in mind, read one chapter per day for the next seven days. Now let us focus on our first goal.

* * *

Money Going to the Wrong Things

There is no denying that Americans, as a whole, are financially well-off. Ironically, perhaps the most vivid picture of American affluence can be best painted by examining the assets of our nation's poor. The following are facts about persons defined as "poor" by the Census Bureau, taken from various government reports:

- Forty-six percent of all poor households actually own their own homes. The average home owned by persons classified as poor by the Census Bureau is a three-bedroom house with one-and-a-half baths, a garage, and a porch or patio.
- Seventy-six percent of poor households have air conditioning. By contrast, 30 years ago, only 36 percent of the entire U.S. population enjoyed air conditioning.
- Only 6 percent of poor households are overcrowded. More than two-thirds have more than two rooms per person.
- The average poor American has more living space than the average individual living in Paris, London, Vienna, Athens, and other cities throughout Europe. (These comparisons are to the average citizens in foreign countries, not to those classified as poor.)
- Nearly three-quarters of poor households own a car; 30 percent own two or more cars.

- Ninety-seven percent of poor households have a color television; over half own two or more color televisions.
- Seventy-eight percent have a VCR or DVD player; 62 percent have cable or satellite TV reception.
- Seventy-three percent own microwave ovens, more than half have a stereo, and a third have an automatic dishwasher.

(Statistics taken from <u>Understanding Poverty in America</u> by Robert E. Rector and Kirk A. Johnson, PhD.: http://www.heritage.org/Research/Welfare/bg1713.cfm)

While these facts definitely don't paint a picture of gross affluence, neither do they convey a message of abject poverty. And remember, these facts are in regard to our nation's poor.

What these facts do portray, however, is a problem that transcends the boundaries between poor, middle-class, and rich Americans. The problem is that of spending money on the wrong things. These facts demonstrate that even many Americans labeled as being poor can acquire material luxuries. However, what these facts do not reveal is the lack of savings, the lack of planning for the future, and the indebtedness that haunts most Americans.

Let us be clear from the outset. None of the material trappings that money can buy are wrong purchases in and of themselves. The very fact that poor Americans have access to things like VCRs and air conditioning demonstrates the strength of our economy and that the American dream is alive and well. However, the question we must ask is whether these material goods are worth the long term cost to our financial well being. Is an extra television in the bedroom worth the potential wealth created through saving and investment? Are two weeks in the Bahamas now worth being able to retire early and travel at leisure without worrying about getting back home to go to work? These questions and ones like them are the ones that Americans are increasingly answering "Yes" to in the false belief that retirement is something to deal with in the distant future, or, even more frighteningly, that retirement planning just somehow magically happens and people are "taken care of".

On top of the idea of spending on the wrong things, perhaps the bigger issue is the method of how most of us choose to purchase these surplus luxuries. There is no denying that much of the satisfaction in working comes from being able to purchase goods or services that bring us pleasure. Who hasn't eased the burden of a long work week with thoughts of the upcoming trip to Hawaii or the upcoming purchase of a hot tub or an expensive night out on the town with friends? The old maxim, "The best things in life are free," may be true, but considering how many hours Americans put in at work and their appetite for spending, few of us actually live by those words.

This being the case, Americans have taken spending to a new level. In antiquity, people purchased primarily out of necessity. The things that they needed that they could not make or acquire on their own were the items that were sought after for purchase. However, as specialization began to set in and marketing products became more common, people began to shift their purchasing habits from buying out of need to buying because of want. In the last 50 years, Americans have shifted their purchasing habits one step further. As incomes have risen and the availability of goods has increased they have gone from purchasing based on wants to purchasing wants on credit.

Nowhere is this phenomenon more apparent than in the skyrocketing credit card debt being amassed by most

14 - The New Mortgage Investment Advisor

Americans. The trend has been going on for decades. According to research obtained by CardWeb.com, a service that tracks credit card trends, the average American household carries over $8,000 in credit card debt.

This $8,000 in credit card debt is staggering on several levels. First, credit card interest rates vary widely. Ranging from roughly 7% to 29%, the time to pay off an $8,000 debt can be vast. Assuming an annual interest rate of 7%, it would take a consumer who committed to a fixed $200 monthly payment (which is well above the minimum monthly payment) 46 months to pay off their debt. Second, while the time to pay off the debt is nearly 4 years, the interest accrued at 7% would amount to $1,136.42. That means with interest paid over the period the actual cost of the debt jumps from $8,000 to $9,136.42. (Table 1.1)

Month	Payment	Interest Paid	Principal Paid	Remaining Balance
1	$200.00	$46.66	$153.34	$7,846.66
13	$200.00	$35.58	$164.42	$5,935.35
25	$200.00	$23.69	$176.31	$3,885.88
37	$200.00	$10.95	$189.05	$1,688.27
46	$136.42	$0.79	$135.63	$0.00
Total	$9,136.42	$1,136.42	$8,000.00	

(Table 1.1)

Keep in mind, as overwhelming as a 46 month period to pay off the debt and an additional $1,136.42 in interest is these numbers assume a low credit card interest rate of 7%. At a rate of 19% the same $8,000 debt paid in $200 monthly installments now takes 64 months instead of 46 to pay off. That's a year and a half increase in time to pay off the debt. Additionally, the interest paid over the 64 months amounts to $4,773.34. That means the total cost of the $8,000 credit card bill from start to finish was actually $12,773.34. (Table 1.2)

Month	Payment	Interest Paid	Principal Paid	Remaining Balance
1	$200.00	$126.66	$73.34	$7,926.66
13	$200.00	$111.45	$88.55	$6,950.59
25	$200.00	$93.08	$106.92	$5,772.04
37	$200.00	$70.90	$129.10	$4,349.00
49	$200.00	$44.12	$155.88	$2,630.75
61	$200.00	$11.78	$188.22	$556.06
64	$173.34	$2.70	$170.64	$0.00
Total	$12,773.34	$4,773.34	$8,000.00	

(Table 1.2)

Neither credit card scenario poses a bright financial outlook for the debtor. Tons of time will be spent paying off purchases that were actually made years ago. Additionally, interest charged will increase the time and cost of transactions like this. Further, the cost of purchasing up front and paying later has huge ramifications in regards to building wealth and preparing for retirement. In the scenarios just given, these consumers sacrificed anywhere from 46 to 64 months and $1,136.42 to $4,773.34. Both the time and money could have been put to use towards preparing for retirement.

Along with credit cards a more recent phenomenon regarding consumer's use of credit has been occurring. The phenomenon revolves around consumer's use of their home equity. With soaring real estate values many Americans have found themselves in a position where they have the ability to pull out cash based on the difference in the value of their home and the amount still owed on the mortgage. This equity is then used, much like a credit card, to finance home remodeling projects, to take fancy vacations, or to pay off other high interest debts.

There is no denying that when compared to credit card debt, home equity use is a far smarter financial decision. First, the interest charged on most home equity loans or lines of credit is far less than that of many credit cards. Second, the interest charged on home equity loans or lines of credit is often tax deductible. However, these positives aside, Americans typical recent use of home equity does nothing to help establish a wealth building strategy or plan for retirement.

Ultimately, regardless of whether we are talking about credit card debt or home equity being consumed, all debts are leading more and more Americans toward the decision to file for bankruptcy. Considered by many to be the last legal and financial resort in dealing with overwhelming consumer debt, the number of Americans who choose this route have been steadily increasing in the past few decades. According to the American Bankruptcy Institute, the number of consumers filing for bankruptcy has increased from almost 300,000 in 1980 to close to 2,000,000 in 2005 (Figure 1.3). While the number alone is staggering, the consequences of filing for bankruptcy for each of these individuals is even more sinister.

First, filing for bankruptcy is not free. This is perhaps the greatest irony regarding most people's perception of bankruptcy. In an attempt to get out of debt, people who file for bankruptcy are subject to filing fees, administrative fees, and other fees required to process their bankruptcy request. Second, not all debts are dischargeable. The popular idea that filing for bankruptcy is a magic, get-out-of-debt free card is false. Certain debts will follow the consumer even after filing for bankruptcy. Third, once a consumer has filed for bankruptcy they cannot file again for years, even if they accrue more debt than they had when they used bankruptcy proceedings to alleviate the burden the first time.

Perhaps the most significant consequences of filing for bankruptcy, however, are that filing for bankruptcy doesn't change consuming habits cultivated over years of purchasing and it destroys ones credit rating which can take decades to rebuild.

* * *

The picture painted for most American's financial future is a mixed one. On the one hand, as we've seen, American's access and ability to afford luxuries is evident. On the other hand, their continued use of credit is not only steadily increasing their debts, it is eating away at their consumable income. More and more Americans are spending more and more of their income simply towards paying off debt. This is not a viable way to plan for the future and retirement.

In the following chapters we will outline how the proper use of home equity and the utilization of the right type of mortgage can dramatically benefit the everyday family in their retirement plan and overall net worth. The strategies that will be explained in their full detail should be reviewed with your financial, tax and legal advisor(s) before implementing them.

18 - The New Mortgage Investment Advisor

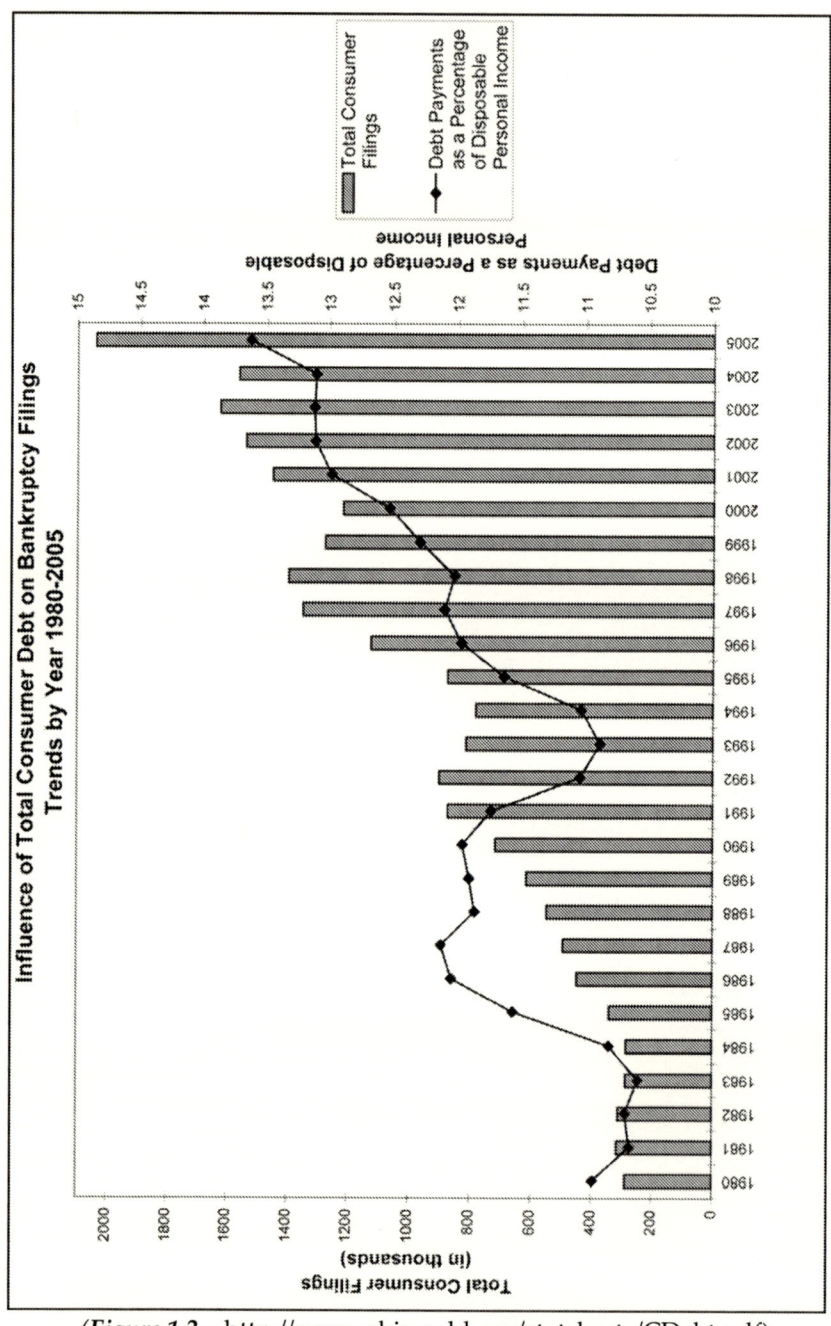

(Figure 1.3 ~ http://www.abiworld.org/statcharts/CDebt.pdf)

Chapter 2
The Traditional Mortgage: Why we do what we do

Chapter 2
The Traditional Mortgage: Why we do what we do

The "American dream" means different things to different people. However, overwhelmingly, people identify the American dream with home ownership. Nothing better signifies success and accomplishment than owning property. Your home is the place where you retreat to at the end of a long day. It is the place where you raise your children and make memories. It anchors us to our communities and is revered in our minds with such sayings as, "Home is where the heart is" and "There is no place like home."

All of these factors provide a huge psychological drive to not only purchase a home, but to aggressively pay off one's mortgage and own the property outright. Further, along with these factors our own nation's history has provided home owners with incentives to do things the way we do.

* * *

Americans and the Conventional "W"

By many accounts the 1920s (often referred to as "The Roaring 20s") were a great time in the lives of most Americans. President Warren G. Harding called for a "return to normalcy" as American soldiers returned home from World War I. President Harding's successor, President Calvin Coolidge, took this return to normalcy one step further and famously announced, "The business of America is business." Americans ate it up. Eager to get back to their pre-war lives, but continuing at a war-time productivity pace, American's standards of living soared. Income levels for many Americans climbed.

With new technology, increased production, availability of credit, and increased income the economic lives of Americans was looking good. All of this led many Americans to purchase homes, solidifying in their minds their accomplishment of the American dream. Unfortunately, the American dream was about to become a nightmare.

Beginning in late 1929 America entered into the Great Depression. Scholars have made careers out of trying to pinpoint the blame for the depression. Some argue the stock market and wild speculation were the culprits. Others assert that government negligence in regulating business led to the economic woes. Still others make differing claims. Regardless of the origin, the depression hit and rank and file Americans were left struggling. Their struggle would worsen with time as their piece of the American dream would be jeopardized.

The assault on the American dream came with increasing bank foreclosures on people's homes. At this time in our nation's history, mortgage lenders could call a loan due at any time while the loan was outstanding. Under normal circumstances, this term was rarely used since it behooved the lender to continue to receive payments with interest on the loan. However, circumstances were anything but normal during the Great Depression. With people in a panic, many withdrew their funds from banks. As banks went into a panic in their attempts to maintain an adequate supply of currency, many called outstanding loans due. This led to further panic as Americans, unable to come up with the full remainder of their home loans, began to see their piece of the American dream foreclosed on. The only Americans who were safe from this prospect of having their loan called in early were people who owned their home outright.

GDP 1920-1940

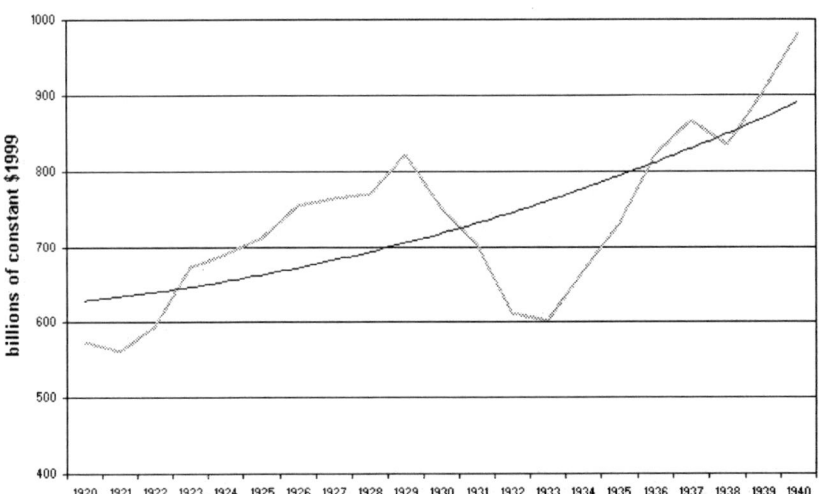

(*Figure 2.1* ~ GDP annual pattern and long-term trend, 1920-40, in billions of constant dollars- based on data in Susan Carter, ed. *Historical Statistics of the US: Millennial Edition* (2006) series Ca9)

It is from this tragic time in our nation's history that the conventional wisdom of owning one's home outright came into existence. This financial line of thinking rests upon two pillars-1) To avoid future loan difficulties it is best to pay off one's home as quickly as possible to make certain that one's loan cannot be called due during hard times or one's interest rate raised when things are difficult and 2) The quicker one pays off their home loan, the quicker one can start using the money that went to one's mortgage payment for other luxuries / investments / living. Further, the quicker one pays off their home loan the quicker one can mark mortgage payments off their list of things to do. Let us examine these two pillars separately.

* * *

American's Loan Woes

The first pillar of American's conventional wisdom regarding owning one's home outright revolves around the various troubles associated with home loans. Most Americans have a limited understanding of the borrowing/lending process and what little they do know usually can be summarized in the following steps: 1) Get a loan from a broker/lender/bank and 2) Spend the next 30 years paying off the loan. While this is not an entirely inappropriate way to view home loans, it is simplistic at best and it definitely accounts for why many Americans have throughout history found themselves in over their heads regarding the terms of their home loans.

The Great Depression was the low point for Americans in terms of loan woes. Taking the place where people live is always tragic. Taking the place where people live when the bulk of the country is struggling just to stay afloat is worse. As a result of this financial fiasco, the way mortgages are structured has changed in this country to protect the interests of home owners. Most significantly, it is now written in as part of the contract of almost all home loans that the loan cannot be called due before the completion of the loan term. This being the case, what happened during the Great Depression, in regards to home ownership and foreclosures, cannot happen again. Unfortunately, especially for the generation of Americans who lived through the Great Depression the psychological damage was done. They had seen the results of foreclosures on people with home loans and their ideas regarding outright home ownership were solidified.

However, while the Great Depression was the low point, there have been other, more recent woes for Americans regarding their home loans. Most memorable for many Baby Boomers were the interest rate hikes of the late 70s/early 80s. During this period, many Americans had either purchased their homes or refinanced their homes with ARM (adjustable rate mortgage) loans. As rates began to rise, many Americans saw their mortgage payments rise, in some cases beyond what they could afford to pay. While nowhere near as bad in scope as the woes brought by the Great Depression, many people were again reminded of the possible pitfalls that could undermine a home owner's pursuit of the American dream. Further, it also reinforced for another generation of Americans the idea that the only way to avoid real estate woes was to own your own home outright.

* * *

Dreams of Financial Freedom

The second pillar that supports the conventional wisdom of Americans regarding their home loans has two facets, but they are inextricably linked. The first facet is that if one pays off their mortgage as quickly as possible then they will be able to allot their mortgage payments to other things. The concept is often colloquially referred to as "found money" because rather than receiving an actual raise in income, money has simply been found in the existing budget which can now be allotted to other things. Especially prominent in the minds of younger Americans with decades left to pay on their mortgage, the thought of being able to allocate a $3,000 a month mortgage payment towards exotic vacations or luxury cars is enticing indeed. Even older Americans are lured by the prospect of finally making those last few years of payments and becoming "financially free" once they can start to spend the money once allotted to their mortgage payment.

The second facet of this pillar refers to the feeling of overwhelming that many Americans experience regarding the decades long payment period involved and the massive debt incurred as a result of taking on a home loan. For many Americans it is a psychological goal to pay off their home simply because they believe it will be one more item they can check off on their to do list.

This second pillar really gets to the heart of Americans desire for both home ownership and wealth creation. Americans eagerly long to pay off their homes because then these homes become theirs in fact. For many Americans this is an inherited psychology that was acquired from their parents and grandparents who lived through the Great Depression. Paying off the mortgage serves them psychologically in that they believe there is one less thing to worry about in their already harried schedules. Additionally, many Americans see a wealth building opportunity in paying aggressively and freeing up mortgage payments to allot to other endeavors. The sad irony is that while these American instincts to build wealth are wonderful, from a financial stand point, paying off one's home can really hinder one's prospects for accumulating wealth. This reality is best illustrated by simply examining the structure of the fixed rate 30 year home loans that many Americans use to pay off their homes.

***
How a 30 Year Home Loan Works

Most Americans intuitively understand the way 30 year home loans work. They fathom that one purchases a loan at the lowest interest rate available and then get to work paying it off. Unfortunately, this understanding does not tell the complete story.

The tyranny of the 30 year fixed loan lies in the psychological comfort of amortization. Amortization simply means the gradual paying off of a debt or loan in regular installments over a period of time. This is the way most loans, including fixed rate 30 year home loans, work. One borrows the amount of their home and then proceeds to pay the debt back in 360 equal payments (30 year loan @ 12 payments per year = 360 equal payments). Again, the main feature of this loan is the psychological comfort it provides. Most Americans purchase their first home early in their adult lives and expect their incomes to increase over time. So, even if the mortgage payment is a little bit of a stretch at first, they believe the process will become easier because their income will grow as they move further up the corporate ladder, yet their mortgage payment will stay the same. Further, as they continue to make monthly payments they believe they are contributing to their future financial well-being by accruing equity in their property.

What many Americans fail to realize is the huge amount of money expended to pay off their home loans. Some assume that a $500,000 loan means 30 years of payments that will amount to $500,000. The more financially adept among us recognize that this would omit the cost of the interest charged on the loan. However, many still do not recognize the full price of a loan, even knowing that interest adds to the cost.

A quick examination of an amortization table will flesh out the true cost of a 30 year fixed home loan. Assuming a loan of $500,000 (approximately the median home price in Los Angeles, CA) at 8% interest one would have a monthly payment of $3,668.82. At this point most Americans simply decide if they are comfortable with this monthly payment and then either take or reject the loan. However, the real cost, as seen through an amortization table, is far greater. (Figure 2.2)

Using the exact same loan, but projecting the payment schedule for 30 years, one sees just how much they are actually paying.

As can be seen in Table 2.3, for the first year of the loan $44,025.87 was spent. Of that money $39,849.05 was spent on interest and $4,176.82 was spent towards paying off the actual loan. The amount toward principal increases slowly month by month until the loan is finally paid off after 30 years.

What jumps out at most people is the huge disparity between the payment to interest and the payment to principal each month. And people are right for noticing that. However, what often goes unnoticed is the total amount of interest paid over the life of the loan. The $500,000 American dream really cost $1,320,776.23 ($500,000 principal paid + $820,776.23 interest paid). By any standard that is a huge mark up. However, whether Americans are not aware of the costs as they enter into loans or they know full well what they are getting into, Americans overwhelmingly choose the 30 year fixed rate loan as the vehicle of choice for servicing their loan needs.

The Traditional Mortgage: Why we do what we do - 29

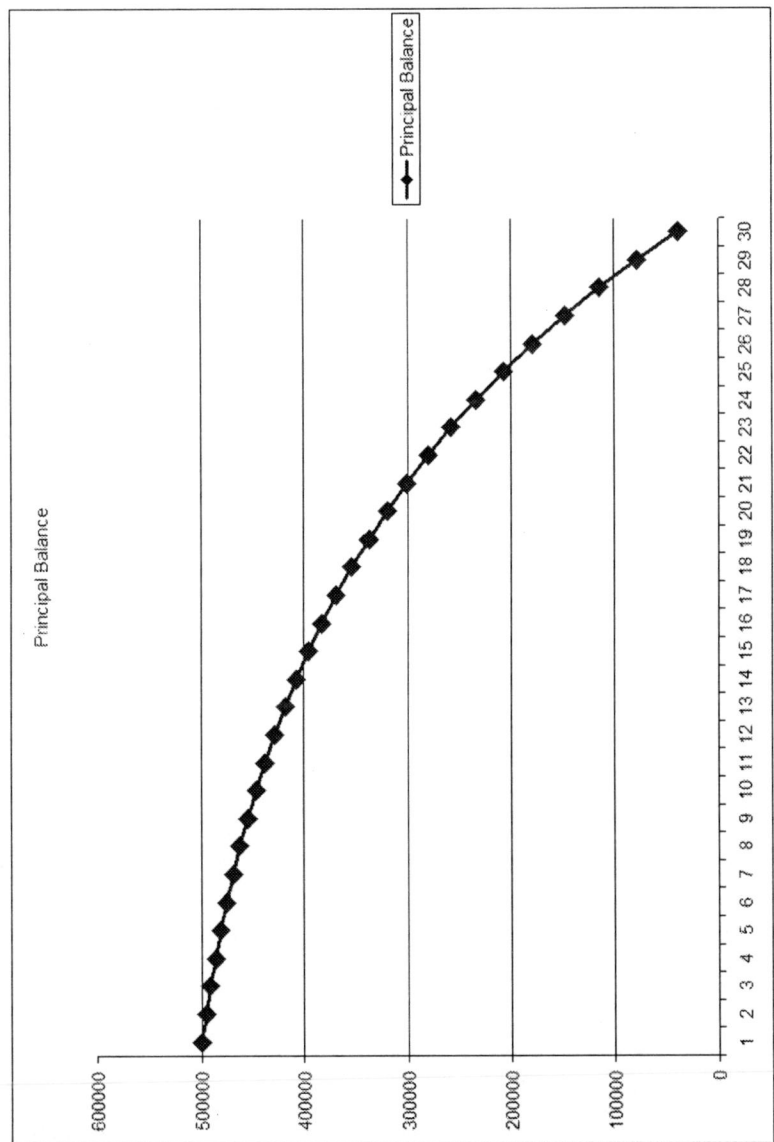

(*Figure 2.2* ~ Amortization table for a 30 Year Fixed Rate Mortgage of $500,000 at 8%.)

30 - The New Mortgage Investment Advisor

Principal borrowed: $500,000.00
Annual Payments: 12 **Total Payments:** 360
Annual interest rate: 8.00% **Periodic interest rate:** 0.6667%
Regular Payment amount: $3668.82 **Final Balloon Payment:** $0.00
The following results are estimates which do not account for values being rounded to the nearest cent. See the amortization schedule for more accurate values.
Total Repaid: $1,320,775.20 **Total Interest Paid:** $820,775.20

End of Year	Cumulative Principal	Cumulative Interest	Principal Balance
1	$4,176.78	$39,849.06	$495,823.22
2	$8,700.23	$79,351.45	$491,299.77
3	$13,599.13	$118,478.39	$486,400.87
4	$18,904.65	$157,198.71	$481,095.35
5	**$24,650.51**	**$195,478.69**	**$475,349.49**
6	$30,873.28	$233,281.76	$469,126.72
7	$37,612.53	$270,568.35	$462,387.47
8	$44,911.14	$307,295.58	$455,088.86
9	$52,815.53	$343,417.03	$447,184.47
10	$61,375.98	$378,882.42	$438,624.02
11	$70,646.93	$413,637.31	$429,353.07
12	$80,687.36	$447,622.72	$419,312.64
13	$91,561.19	$480,774.73	$408,438.81
14	$103,337.52	$513,024.24	$396,662.48
15	$116,091.27	$544,296.33	$383,908.73
16	$129,903.58	$574,509.86	$370,096.42
17	$144,862.29	$603,576.99	$355,137.71
18	$161,062.56	$631,402.56	$338,937.44
19	$178,607.45	$657,883.51	$321,392.55
20	$197,608.58	$682,908.22	$302,391.42
21	$218,186.79	$706,355.85	$281,813.21
22	$240,472.98	$728,095.50	$259,527.02
23	**$264,608.90**	**$747,985.42**	**$235,391.10**
24	$290,748.10	$765,872.06	$209,251.90
25	$319,056.83	$781,589.17	$180,943.17
26	$349,715.17	$794,956.67	$150,284.83
27	$382,918.14	$805,779.54	$117,081.86
28	$418,876.94	$813,846.58	$81,123.06
29	$457,820.31	$818,929.05	$42,179.69
30	$500,000.00	$820,779.23	$0.00

(Table 2.3)

* * *
A Better Way

Even if we are aware of the huge costs of a 30 year fixed mortgage, most of us do not see any possible alternative. Renting, over the long haul, seems foolish because home prices continue to rise and rent checks do nothing to establish equity. However, few of us can afford to purchase a home with cash. It would seem that huge monthly payments that end up often amounting to more than double the loan value are simply the price of doing business. But what if there were a better way?

For many reasons, some historical, some traditional, some psychological, Americans prefer 30 year fixed mortgages. However, the historical reasons for owning one's home outright do not hold water today. Lenders are not going to foreclose like they did during the Great Depression. Further, if runaway variable interest rates are what feeds American's fears, they can be assuaged by looking at the historical rates of the 30 year U.S. Treasury Bond (a good representation of the interest rates for the average home loan). Historically these rates have been below 7.5% for the past 200 years (yet we all remember the high rates of 70's and 80's)! The simple point regarding our historical reasons for doing what we do is that what worked for our grandparents and our parents does not necessarily work for us.

Traditionally we are told to pay our mortgage and own our home outright. Psychologically we are comfortable with the idea of a steady, continuous payment for 30 years. But at the end of 30 years we own a house free and clear but all of the value is locked up in the equity. Again, what if there was a better way?

e New Mortgage Investment Advisor

The good news is that wealthy Americans have been practicing this better way for some time. In fact, the wealthy in America do something so counterintuitive to most Americans that even revealing their secret will not convince some. The better way that we are talking about is **never paying off your home loan!**

How could this be possible? Why would anyone want to do this? Can the wisdom of our grandparents and parents be so wrong? To understand this one must understand the way our tax system operates and the nature of compound interest.

Chapter 3
Building a Better Mousetrap

Chapter 3
Building a Better Mousetrap

For all the great products, ideas, and businesses Americans have created, ironically we tend to be a fairly risk averse people, at least in regards to our personal investments. Everyone seems to have (or knows someone who has) some "cousin" who lost his shirt in some fly by night, get rich quick scheme. Further, some of our most popular axioms- sayings that we raise our kids with and which continue to inform our thinking throughout our adult lives- demonstrate our fiscal conservativeness. We've all heard of the warning to "look before you leap". Financially this is in the back of most of our minds as we consider making purchases sight unseen. Based on this adage, few of us would ever consider purchasing a used car without having seen the vehicle in person (let alone taking it out for a test drive). Another popular maxim (and one that most of us were raised on) is "a penny saved is a penny earned". Cruelly, it is this very maxim that often leads Americans in poor financial directions.

The wisdom of maxims is that they tend to be self-evident. This is clearly the case regarding the concept of saving money to earn money. However, the problem with this (and many maxims) is that their simplicity often doesn't convey the whole picture. It is true that saving a penny means a penny has been earned. However, is it possible that people are confused by the simplicity of the statement to the point that they miss better opportunities that may not be as seemingly apparent?

The point we're getting at is this- the wisdom of saving a penny, thereby earning a penny is self-evident. However, what if there were multiple ways to save a penny? Are all methods of saving equal? If all methods are not equal, how does one go about discerning the differences and making the best decision?

Clearly there are multiple ways to save and all methods are not equal. This leaves us with the problem of discerning the differences and making the best decision. Tragically, many Americans are not choosing the best method.

* * *

Expert Economists and their View on the "Conventional Wisdom"

In August 2006 the Federal Reserve Bank of Chicago via three nationally recognized economists published a paper that studied the possibility that many American households could realize significant financial gains if they performed a tax arbitrage by reducing their additional mortgage payments (the payment above and beyond the required monthly payment) and putting that money into tax-deferred accounts. Simply put, the study concludes that in many instances households that are diligently conforming to the conventional wisdom we discussed at length in the previous chapter of making extra payments towards their mortgage obligation and striving to own their home free and clear early are making a poor financial decision by doing this rather than saving the money in a tax-deferred investment vehicle. The traditional fears relating to debt and risk are cited as the self-reported reasons why most people do not consider an alternate strategy in order to best save for retirement.

The Tradeoff between Mortgage Prepayments and Tax-Deferred Retirement Savings

Gene Amrominy[†] Jennifer Huangz[‡] Clemens Sialmx[§]

August, 2006

Abstract

We show that a significant number of households can perform a tax arbitrage by cutting back on their additional mortgage payments and increasing their contributions to tax-deferred accounts (TDA). Using data from the Survey of Consumer Finances, we show that about 38% of U.S. households that are accelerating their mortgage payments instead of saving in tax-deferred accounts are making the wrong choice. For these households, reallocating their savings can yield a mean benefit of 11 to 17 cents per dollar, depending on the choice of investment assets in the TDA. In the aggregate, these misallocated savings are costing U.S. households as much as 1.5 billion dollars per year. Finally, we show empirically that this inefficient behavior is unlikely to be driven by liquidity considerations and that self-reported debt aversion and risk aversion variables explain to some extent the preference for paying off debt obligations early and hence the propensity to forgo our proposed tax arbitrage.

(*Figure 3.1* ~ Abstract from Pg 2 of the Federal Reserve Bank of Chicago's paper on The Tradeoff Between Mortgage Prepayments and Tax-Deferred Retirement Savings.)

The data provided in the study is pretty damning. Based on their figures, the economists make a startling assertion: "Depending on the choice of the investment asset in the TDA (tax deferred account), the mean gain from such a reallocation ranges between 11 and 17 cents per dollar of 'mis-allocated savings.'" (Fed Bank of Chicago- *The Tradeoff Between Mortgage Prepayments and Tax Deferred Retirement Savings*, page 2) Missing out on that kind of money is an investment debacle! Further, the tragedy is compounded because Americans are not simply missing an opportunity because they are unable to take advantage of it, rather, Americans are in a position to take advantage of an opportunity but they bypass it for a less efficient transaction! Individual households are missing out on a veritable fortune simply due to asset misallocation. In fact, the study concluded that if these poor investment choices were remedied and Americans would reallocate assets away from accelerated mortgage payments to tax-deferred accounts then American households could realize collectively a savings of as much as **1.5 billion dollars** per year. (Fed Bank Chicago- *The Tradeoff Between Mortgage Prepayments and Tax-Deferred Retirement Saving,* pg. 2) (Figure 3.1)

***

Alternatives to Paying Down Mortgages

Again, there are multiple ways to save a penny. As just outlined, the conventional wisdom asserts that the best way to save a penny is to pay down one's mortgage, thereby saving on future interest payments and concluding one's mortgage obligation early. Many Americans, for a multitude of reasons (aversion to debt, fear of risk, relative ease of participation, etc.) choose this method. However, the downside of this is that most American's primary tax shelter (their mortgage interest) is aggressively depleted and the accrued equity earns zero interest. Clearly, for many Americans, the smarter financial decision is to forgo additionally mortgage payments and save money in a separate account. However, what if there was a strategy that not only performed a tax arbitrage but accelerated the growth of one's investments by unlocking equity to be used for gain? One potential possibility is the utilization of interest only loans.

* * *

Interest only loans are loans that allow the borrower to pay only the interest portion of the payment, rather than the traditional interest + principal payment. This allows the person with an interest only loan the opportunity to increase their monthly cash flow due to a lower monthly payment. It is this extra cash flow that can provide dynamic wealth building opportunities. An example to demonstrate is in order.

Assume that you are a homeowner looking to refinance your house. The value of your house is $500,000 and you are looking for a $400,000 loan. At this point you are thinking about following the conventional wisdom and getting a traditional 30 year fixed loan. You shop various lenders, compare rates, closing costs, and fees and settle on a 30 year fixed rate mortgage at 5.77% interest (all rates based on real offerings at bankrate.com April 2007). Once the loan documents are signed and the process complete, you can anticipate a monthly mortgage payment of $2,339. This is amortization which simply means the gradual paying off of a debt in regular intervals. (Figure 3.2)

The good news is that since the debt is amortized this payment will never go up for the life of the loan. The bad news, unfortunately, is two-fold. First, this payment will never decrease for the life of the loan. The second downside, that equity is not an interest earning growing asset, requires a more extended explanation.

Amortization Chart

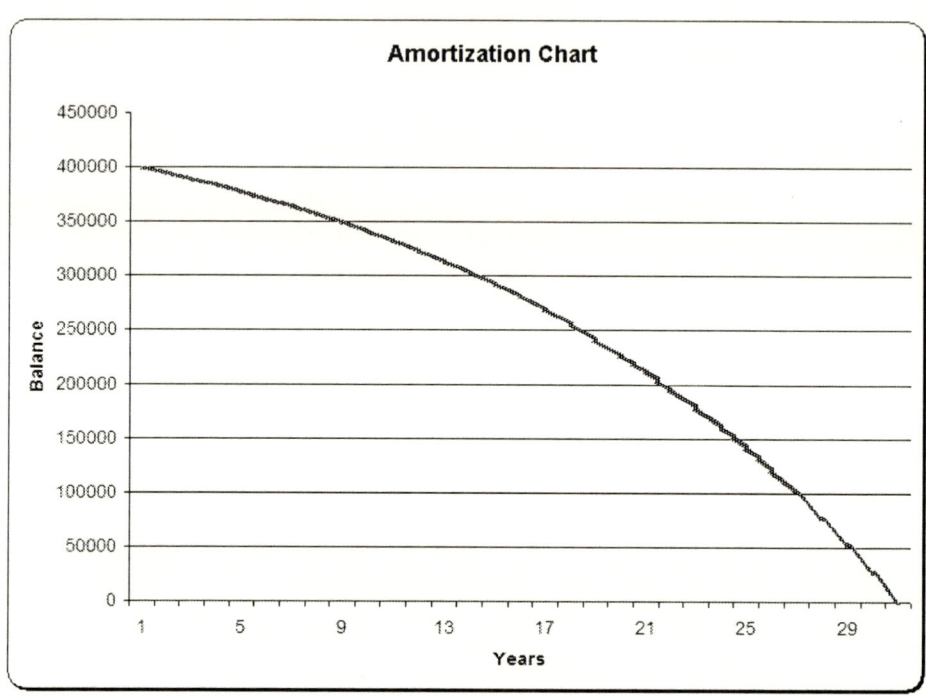

(*Figure 3.2* ~ Amortization Chart for $400,000 debt at 5.77% interest for 30 years.)

* * *

Equity Accrual: An Untapped and Often Wasted Resource

Over time, the slow and steady payment of a 30 year fixed rate mortgage builds equity provided your real estate doesn't go down in value due to outside conditions such as the general state of real estate market affairs. The potential is that every penny of principal paid towards the loan amount equals a penny of equity. However, while this is a sought after goal of most American homeowners, the tragedy is that equity has three major shortcomings. First, equity is not liquid. Unlike an investment account, equity cannot simply be withdrawn and utilized, rather,

Amortization Chart

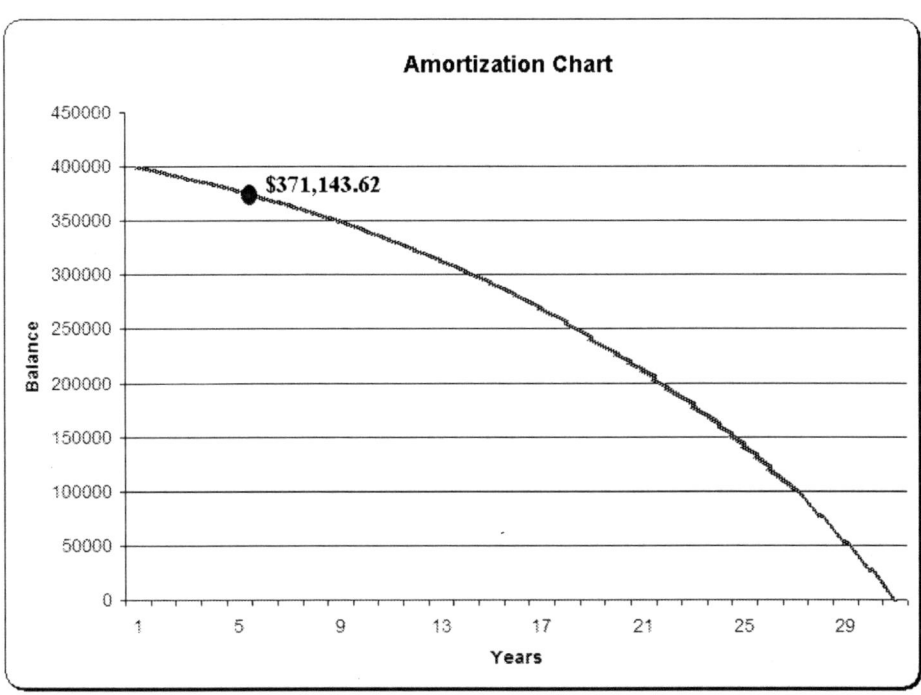

(Figure 3.3 ~ 5 years in on a $400,000 30 year fixed rate loan at 5.77% would result in $28,856.38 in equity if the property did not appreciate or depreciate. This $28,856.38 would be earning a 0% rate of return no matter if the housing market rises or falls.)

it requires either a loan against the existing equity or a credit line against the equity. Both of these options take time, resources, and credit worthiness for qualification by a lender to grant you access to your equity. Second, equity is ephemeral in that while it most often builds up over time (both through payment of principal on the loan and appreciation of property values), it is possible for equity to diminish over time (through the depreciation of property values). This is a frightening reality considering how many Americans aggressively pay down their home loans assuming that the value of the equity in their homes will

Amortization Chart

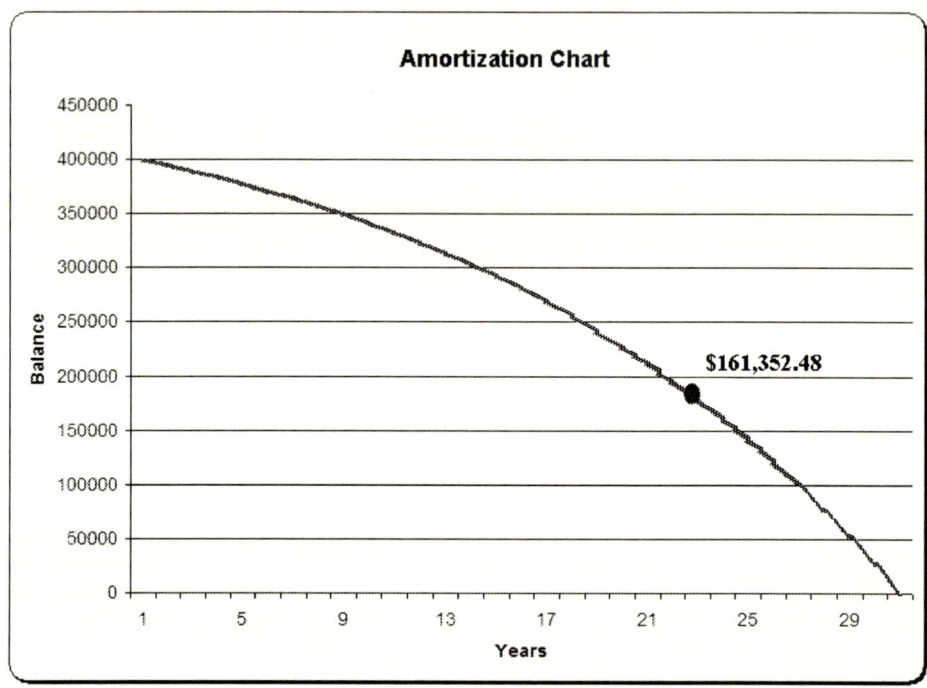

(Figure 3.4 ~ 23 years in on a $400,000 30 year fixed rate loan at 5.77% would result in $238,647.52 in equity if the property did not appreciate or depreciate. This $238,647.52 would be earning a 0% rate of return no matter if the housing market rises or falls.)

never diminish. Third, equity earns no interest. The equity that is built up by Americans is simply a number that does nothing. So, even if a person were to pay off their home and have the entire value of their home locked away as equity, that entire home value is not an interest earning growing asset.

A tangible example of this can be derived from our previous scenario involving the $400,000 30 year fixed rate loan. In the scenario our monthly payment was fixed at $2,339. After 5 years of faithfully making payments you still would owe $371,143.62 on the original $400,000 mortgage. The good news is that you would have $28,856.38 in equity from paying down the principal of the loan. The bad news is that same $28,856 would be sitting fallow earning nothing. (Figure 3.3)

Sadly, the picture does not get much rosier as time goes on. 23 years later, well over 2/3s of the payments have been made, yet you would still owe $161,352.48 on the original $400,000 loan. The good news again is that you would have $238,647.52 in equity, but, just like at the 5 year point, it would still be earning no additional interest. (Figure 3.4)

* * *

The Difference with an Interest Only Loan

The huge wealth potential becomes evident using the same $400,000 loan example when we substitute the 30 year fixed rate loan product for an interest only loan. Taking the same loan amount ($400,000) and assuming an interest rate of 5.49% (again, rates are based on bankrate.com April 2007) the total monthly payment would be $1,830. Subtracting the difference between the fixed payment ($2,339) and the interest only payment ($1,830) gives us a monthly cash savings of $509. This monthly cash savings amounts to $6,108 per year. (Figure 3.5)

Year	Interest Only at 5.49%	30 year Fixed Rate at 5.77 %	Monthly Cash Flow Savings*	Annual Cash Flow Savings*
1	$1,830	$2,339	$509	$6,108
2	$1,830	$2,339	$509	$6,108
3	$1,830	$2,339	$509	$6,108
4	$1,830	$2,339	$509	$6,108
5	$1,830	$2,339	$509	$6,108
Total 5 Year Cash Flow Savings = $30,540			

(*Figure 3.5*)

***
The Rule of 72

The reason one might want to take their principal portion of their dollars and invest them outside of the walls of their home is because of the power of compounding interest. In fact, the key to dynamic wealth generation is compound interest. Everyone understands the concept of an investment earning interest. Interest is simply the fee paid on borrowed money. If one lends money the return on investment most commonly comes in the form of interest. If one owns stocks or mutual funds (equities) that appreciate over time, the gains on this type of investment are referred to as rate of return. For the sake of explanation we will refer to rate of return on equities and interest simply as the later, interest. The concept that often eludes many people is the difference between simple interest and compounding interest.

Simple interest is calculated by taking the amount of principal (the amount of money invested) and multiplying it by the interest rate. For example, if one was to invest $10,000 at 8% interest earned annually, to calculate the simple interest earned one would simply multiply $10,000 (the principal invested) by 8% (the interest rate). The result would be $800 interest earned for a grand total of $10,800 (principal and interest combined).

An extra $800 is wonderful, but the big gains are found when interest compounds. Compound interest refers to the idea that when interest is calculated it is based not just on the original principal, but also on any interest that has been added to the principal. Returning to our example of investing $10,000 at 8% interest (assuming the interest is paid to the principal at the end of the year); if we decided to let the money be invested for a second year, the principle of compounding comes into play. Rather than 8% interest accruing on the $10,000 investment, we are now talking about 8% interest accruing on $10,800 (the amount of the principal and the interest that has been added to the principal). The result of compounding would yield a total of $11,664 ($10,000 original principal + $800 accrued interest x 8% interest = $11,664).

The ultimate objective in any investment is to multiply your monies. The primary question every investor wants to know is how long is it going to take my money to double. For those of us who do not want to be bothered with some long formula, one can calculate how long it will take to double their investment using what is known as the Rule of 72. The Rule is based on the simple premise that one can figure out how many years it will take to double their investment by taking the number 72 and dividing it by the interest rate their investment is earning. The result of the computation is the approximate length of time it will take to double one's principal.

For example, using our $10,000 at 8% interest we can simply take the interest rate and divide it into 72 to figure out roughly how long it will take to double our money. So, using the Rule of 72, we would take our interest rate, 8, and divide it into 72. The result is 9 which means it would take approximately 9 years at 8% interest to double our investment. In the case of our example, our $10,000 would grow to $20,000 in 9 years at 8% interest.

The beauty of the Rule of 72 lies in its simplicity. It is simple because there is no long formula to memorize. Simply divide 72 by whatever interest rate you are earning and you can determine the approximant length of time it takes to double your money. Bear in mind when using the

Rule of 72 that the performance of investments fluctuates over time and as a result the actual time it will take an investment to double in value cannot be predicted with any certainty. Additionally, the Rule of 72 does not take into account any taxes, fees assessed with any particular investment or risks that might be involved. For those basic reasons, the Rule of 72 is used to approximate the time for your investment to double.

The power of compound interest can be best seen when comparing the growth of $100,000 at 4% and at 8%. Using the Rule of 72, we know that an investment growing at 4% will take approximately 18 years to double. Let us take an example of a 29 year old woman with $100,000 that she wants to invest. At 4%, her investment will double around every 18 years. Assuming she plans to retire at age 65, her $100,000 has had the chance to double to $200,000 at age 47 and then the $200,000 has had the chance to double to $400,000 by age 65. No matter how you look at it, growing your money from $100,000 to $400,000 is good. But let's say that our 29 year old woman knows a little something about investing. Let's say instead of earning 4%, she knows how to earn 8% (something that will be explained in greater detail in chapter 7). According to the Rule of 72, that money will take around 9 years to double. So now at age 65, her $100,000 doubled to $200,000 at age 38, her $200,000 doubled to $400,000 at age 47, her $400,000 doubled to $800,000 at age 56, and her $800,000 doubled to $1,600,000 at age 65. That is a difference of 1.2 million on the same investment! (Figure 3.6)

Armed with the knowledge of the Rule of 72, let's look back at our interest only loan.

The Rule of 72

$100,000 to invest

4% Growth 18 Years to Double		8% Growth 9 Years to Double	
Age 29	$100,000	Age 29	$100,000
		Age 38	$200,000
Age 47	$200,000	Age 47	$400,000
		Age 56	$800,000
Age 65	$400,000	Age 65	$1,600,000

(*Figure 3.6*)

* * *

Unlike the fixed rate loan, the interest only loan pays nothing towards principal. Therefore, no equity is being built based on mortgage payments. However, the amount that is dedicated to paying the principal in the fixed loan is now free to be invested because of using the interest only product. The difference in wealth accumulation is staggering.

This $6,108 per year cash flow, invested at 8% interest (Chapter 7 will explain why and how we use a growth rate of 8%), grows to $37,649.05 in 5 years. Remembering the 5 year point in our 30 year fixed rate example, the equity accumulated was $28,856.38. Therefore, by opting for the interest only loan and investing the difference between the fixed and interest only monthly payments at an 8% rate of return would provide a gain of $8,792.67! (Figure 3.7)

48 - The New Mortgage Investment Advisor

Interest Only Loan

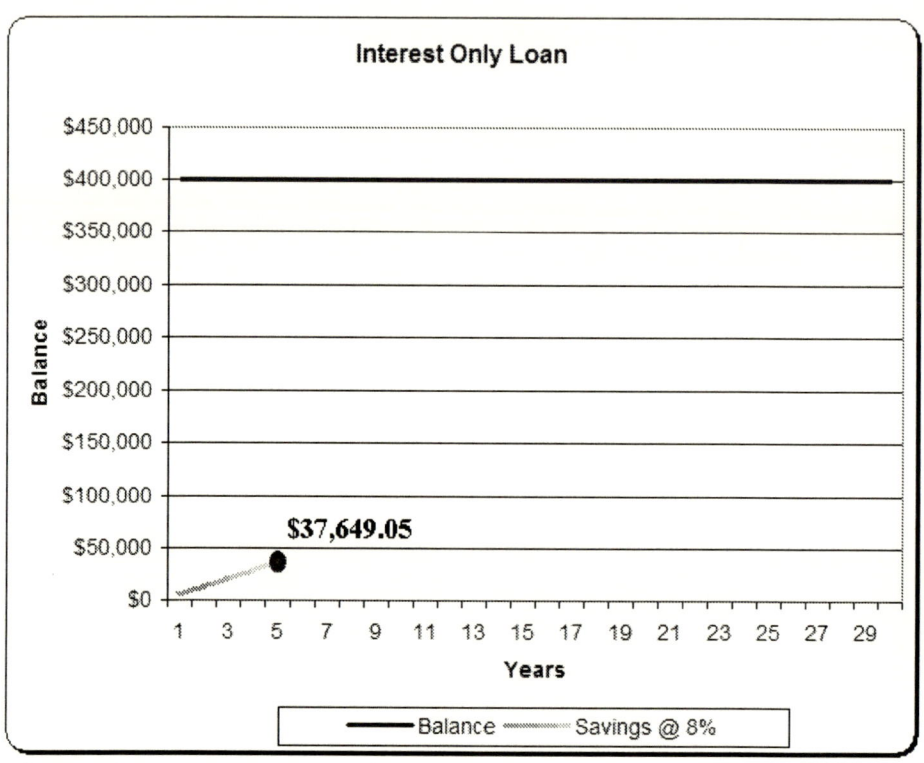

[Chart showing Balance over 30 Years with flat Balance line at $400,000 and Savings @ 8% curve marked at $37,649.05 around year 5]

(Figure 3.7 ~ 5 years in on a $400,000 Interest Only loan with the monthly cash flow savings of $509 invested at 8% would result in $37,649.05 in savings.)

The cash difference alone is astounding. However, perhaps the best part is that this difference required no additional payment on the part of the investor. The difference comes simply as a result of investing the principal payment and allowing the interest to compound versus settling for the principal payment to merely accumulate and sit.

Extending the example out over the course of the loan only further demonstrates the dynamic difference in wealth accumulation between using a fixed interest rate loan and an interest only loan. At the end of the 30 year fixed rate loan the $400,000 is paid off and you own your home free and clear with $400,000 in equity earning zero interest. However, allowing the cash flow difference to continue to compound for the full 30 year loan term using the interest only loan results in a gain of $763,650.25! (Figure 3.8) At this point you would still owe the original $400,000 on the loan (you have only been paying the interest, hence the name interest only loan) but after paying off that $400,000 you would have an extra $363,650.25 left over. With no additional investment amount and simply bucking the conventional wisdom of using a 30 year fixed interest rate loan to opt for the interest only loan you would have almost doubled your investment dollar. To be clear, at the time of the writing of this book, there isn't a 30 year interest only loan. The longest one that we are aware of is a 15 year interest only loan. When this strategy is employed, it is generally recommended that a 3, 5, 7, or 10 year interest only loan is obtained and at the end of the 3, 5, 7, or 10 years a new interest only loan is obtained and the program is continued. For the sake of clarity on this example, we are assuming that the loan remains constant for the 30 year term.

These examples more than demonstrate the financial advantage of growing the cash flow difference in principal payments in an investment account versus settling for an amortized fixed interest payment. However, for those who are still convinced that it is important to pay one's mortgage as fast as possible, the interest only loan still has something to offer.

If one opts for the 30 year fixed rate loan the only way to decrease the 30 year loan period is to increase the monthly payment. Using our example again, this would mean that to decrease the 30 year loan period the borrower would have to

Interest Only Loan

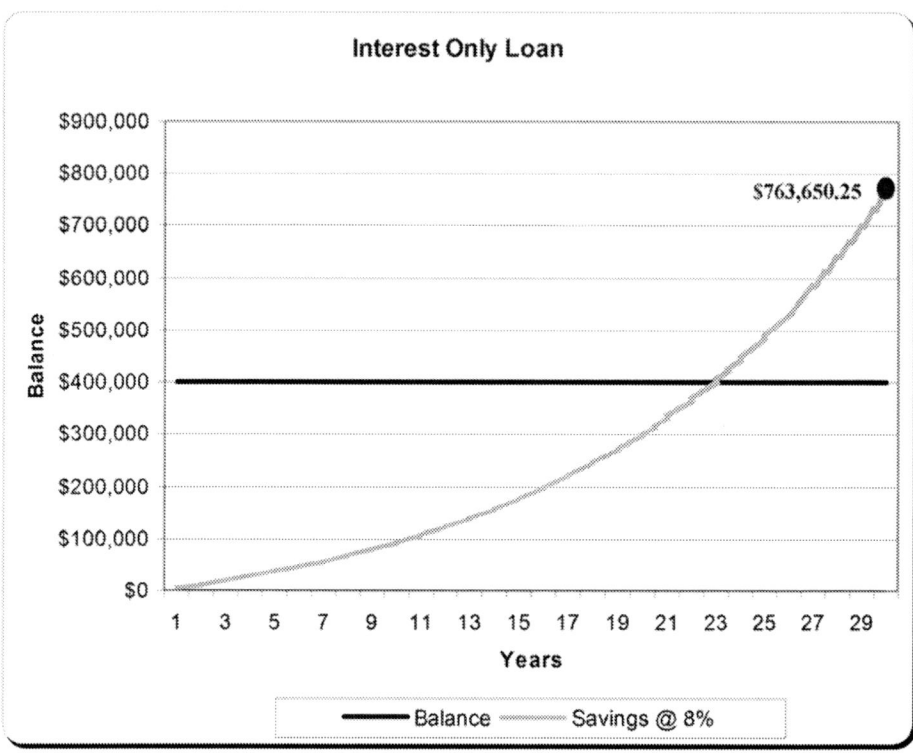

(*Figure 3.8* ~ 30 years in on a $400,000 Interest Only loan with the monthly cash flow savings of $509 invested at 8% would result in $763,650.25 in savings with the original $400,000 principal still due.)

find a way to increase their monthly payment of $2,339 by an amount significant enough to decrease the loan term. $2,339 a month is already a significant amount of money, but assuming one could manage to spend an extra $100 per month toward loan principal prepayment they would lower the 30 year term by approximately 3 years. This means that they would have to come up with an extra $1,200 per year for 27 years ($100 per month x 12= $1,200 per year. 3 years eliminated from a 30 year loan = 27 year loan term) for a grand total of $32,400 in extra payments ($1,200 x 27= $32,400). This $32,400 is in addition to the regular monthly payment that must be paid. That's a lot of money to simply eliminate 3 years off of a 30 year loan term!

If one wanted to increase the payment to $250 a month, the 30 year loan term would decrease by a little more than 6 years. Again, one needs to weigh the costs. At $250 per month, one would be spending an extra $3,000 per year to speed up the term of their 30 year loan. To lower the term of the loan by a little more than 6 years $3,000 would have to be paid every year of the loan for a grand total of $72,000. This $72,000 is in addition to the regular monthly payment. Further, this $72,000 earns no further interest once used as prepayment toward principal. Unfortunately, it simply increases the speed in which equity is accumulated.

The extra payments required to decrease the payment term of a fixed rate interest loan makes the strategy cost prohibitive. However, using an interest only loan can potentially lower the payment term with no additional payments required. Returning to our interest only loan example, you'll remember that if one was investing the cash flow difference between the fixed rate loan and the interest only loan ($509 per month) at 8% interest then they would have a gain of $763,650.25 at the end of the 30 year loan term. However, interestingly, if early termination of the loan was a person's goal, this could be done faster and far cheaper than our fixed rate examples demonstrated using an interest only loan. Keeping in mind the original loan amount of $400,000, one would simply need to calculate how long it would take for our $509 per month investment at 8% interest to compound to the loan amount of $400,000. It just so happens that this goal is reached during year 23 of the loan ($509 @ 8% interest x 23 years = $404,140.56). Sometimes referred to as the "Freedom Point", at this point you could withdraw the funds from your investment and

52 - The New Mortgage Investment Advisor

pay off the total of your $400,000 principal balance and remove all your debt obligation in regards to your home loan. (Figure 3.9) So, not only does utilizing the interest only loan provide the opportunity to pay off one's loan faster than the fixed loan, it does so **without the additional monthly payments.** This means both time and money are saved.

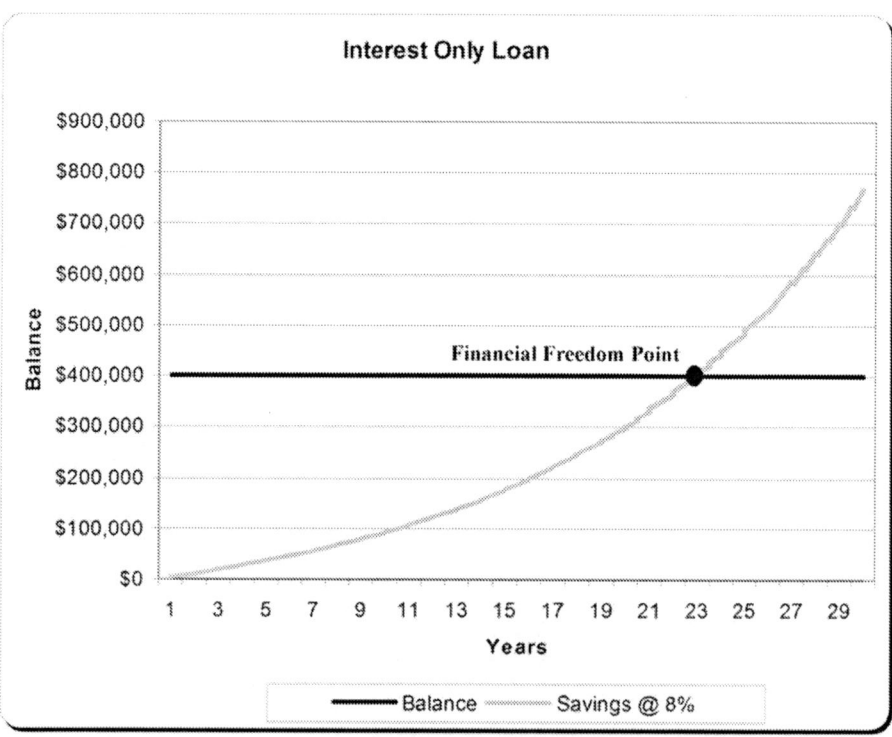

(*Figure 3.9* ~ The Financial Freedom Point is reached in year 23.)

***
Tax Savings and Cash Out with an Interest Only Loan

At this juncture we've steadily compared the results of utilizing an interest only loan versus a 30 year fixed rate loan. When compared, the interest only loan grants significant wealth accumulation potential that the fixed rate loan just can't provide. However, two more additional benefits can potentially be garnered from choosing an interest only loan. The first is increased tax savings off of mortgage interest. The second is the potential for getting cash out of your investment early.

First, let us examine how tax deductions work. In the United States, we have a graduated income tax. In other words, everyone does not pay the same percentage in taxes, rather, the percentage paid is based on the amount earned. Lower income Americans pay a smaller percentage of their income in taxes and the percentages increase through various brackets as income increases. Currently, there are 6 income brackets that determine one's Federal marginal tax rate (many states have an income tax as well). The brackets are as follows: 10%, 15%, 25%, 28%, 33%, and 35%. Individuals (or married couples filing jointly) reach these different brackets as their income levels rise.

The marginal tax rate is in regards to the brackets that we just listed previously. Whatever the highest tax bracket, based on their income, an individual is in is their marginal tax rate.

The effective tax rate is the rate at which the totality of their income actually gets taxed at. The marginal and effective tax rates are not the same and this is usually where the confusion lies. An example will provide clarity.

If you lived in California and earned $100,000 and filed your income tax as married filling jointly, you would have a marginal tax rate of 34.3% (25% Federal bracket & 9.3% State bracket.). However, this does not mean that you will pay 34.3% of $100,000 as your income tax obligation. To reach the 34.3% marginal tax rate, you had to earn enough income to be in the 10% marginal tax bracket. Your income up to the point where you exceed the marginal tax bracket of 10% is taxed at 10%. The next portion of your income puts you in the 15% tax bracket. The last portion of your income pushed you into the 25% Federal marginal tax bracket (the same effect was happening with your state bracket but at different points and at different percentages). The point being made is that all of your income is not charged at the marginal tax rate, rather, your income is charged at differing rates up to the point that your income exceeds the maximum for that tax bracket. This means that your effective tax rate will be lower than the marginal tax rate. Further it also means that any sort of tax deductions you receive will be deducted at the highest marginal tax rate you pay at. So, returning to our example, if you are in the 34.3% marginal tax bracket, and you had a deductible mortgage interest of $1, then you would receive a 34.3 cent tax savings. Even though some of your income was taxed at 10%, 15%, and so on, you received a tax savings based on the highest marginal tax bracket you were in.

Now that the marginal tax bracket system is understood, let us consider another example revolving around a homeowner named Jane. Jane is 45 years old and has been steadily paying off her home year after year. She is single with no children and has very little retirement savings. She currently has a mortgage at 6.25% interest and she is making a monthly mortgage payment of $844.05

(higher than what is required). With only around $78,000 left to pay on her loan she is set to be finished with her loan in only 11 more years. At this point, Jane could simply stay the course, pay off her loan, and be about her business. The conventional wisdom asserts that this is the proper financial decision. However, doing so could potentially have huge financial repercussions.

Fortunately, Jane is not bound by the conventional wisdom and is open to considering differing financial strategies. This being the case, she considers an interest only loan. However, unlike our previous examples, Jane also considers not just refinancing the remaining principal of her current loan. Jane also considers tapping into the equity she has accumulated that is simply sitting fallow earning no interest. So, Jane is ultimately looking to refinance her original loan amount of $77,954, borrow a portion of her accrued home equity, and attempt to keep the monthly mortgage payment the same or less than what she is currently paying. To evaluate the possibility of all these conditions being met we must examine Jane's total financial picture relating to her mortgage and her mortgage interest tax deduction.

Since this scenario that is being shared is based on a real life client scenario (her name has been changed), her accurate situation will be used. Jane is in a 32.80% marginal tax bracket (this is Federal and State bracket combined). With a loan balance of $77,954 and making monthly payments of $844.05 she will make a total mortgage payment this year of $10,129. Of that $10,129 total payment $5,410 is applied to the loan principal and $4,719 is interest. Since Jane is in a 32.80% marginal tax bracket her mortgage interest tax write off amounts to a $1,548 tax savings ($4,719 x 32.80% = $1,548). This means that after tax savings, her net mortgage payment for the year was $8,581 ($10,129 - $1,548 = $8,581).

If Jane continues with her current loan her monthly payment will remain fixed at $844.05 as will her gross mortgage annual payment of $10,129. However, her net mortgage payment after tax savings will actually **increase** slightly over the next 10 years. This is because as more and more of her monthly payment is applied to the loan principal, she has less loan interest to use as a tax write off. (Figure 3.10)

At this juncture, having assessed her situation, Jane considers an interest only loan (assumed at 6.25%) for her refinancing needs. Additionally, she recognizes that she can borrow $100,000 of her home's equity to invest and still have a lower net payment after tax benefits. This is how it works.

Jane's new interest only loan will be for $183,000. This figure is reached by adding in the current value of the loan she is refinancing ($77,954), withdrawing some of the existing equity she has accumulated in her home ($100,000), and approximating the closing costs for purchasing the new loan ($4,575). At 6.25% interest, Jane's new monthly payment will be $953.13. This is a $109.08 monthly increase or a $1,309 yearly increase in mortgage payments. So, to compare, Jane spent $10,129 (before tax savings) a year (principal and interest) in her original loan. Jane spent $11,437 (before tax savings) a year in her interest only loan.

Before tax savings Jane is paying more on her interest only loan than her fixed interest rate loan. However, after tax savings the tables turn in favor of the interest only loan. Of the $10,129 yearly mortgage payment in her original loan, only $4,719 was interest. After calculating her tax savings ($4,719 x 32.80% = $1,548), Jane's net yearly mortgage payment after tax was $8,581. In regards to Jane's interest

Loan Balance	$77,954
Payment Being Made	$844.05
Interest Rate	6.25%
Loan Type	15 Yr Fixed
Marginal Tax Bracket	32.80%

Year	Loan Balance	Principal Payment	Interest Payment	Total Annual Payment	Tax Savings	Net-Payment After Tax
1	$72,544	$5,410	$4,719	$10,129	$1,548	$8,581
2	$66,787	$5,758	$4,371	$10,129	$1,434	$8,695
3	$60,659	$6,128	$4,001	$10,129	$1,312	$8,816
4	$54,136	$6,522	$3,606	$10,129	$1,183	$8,946
5	$47,195	$6,942	$3,187	$10,129	$1,045	$9,083
6	$39,807	$7,388	$2,740	$10,129	$899	$9,230
7	$31,943	$7,863	$2,265	$10,129	$743	$9,386
8	$23,574	$8,369	$1,759	$10,129	$577	$9,552
9	$14,667	$8,908	$1,221	$10,129	$401	$9,728
10	$5,186	$9,480	$648	$10,129	$123	$9,916
11		$5,186	$99	$10,129	$32	$5,253
TOTAL		$77,954	$28,617	$106,571	$9,386	$97,185

(Figure 3.10 ~ Tax savings assume a state and federal marginal tax bracket of 32.8% multiplied by the interest payment. Net payment after tax equals the Total Payment less the Tax Savings.)

only loan, her total yearly mortgage payment is $11,437. However, since all of that payment is interest, the tax savings are far more significant. Calculating the tax savings ($11,437 x 32.80% = $3,751) gives Jane a net yearly mortgage payment after tax of $7,686. This is an after tax savings of $895 over her original loan. Additionally, unlike Jane's original loan where the tax savings decreases each year because the amount of interest paid decreases, the interest only loan will have a tax savings of $3,751 every year. The tax savings never decreases because the payment is always 100% interest.

58 - The New Mortgage Investment Advisor

	Loan Balance				$183,000	
	Payment Being Made				$953.13	
	Interest Rate				6.25%	
	Loan Type				Interest Only	
	Marginal Tax Bracket				32.80%	

Year	Loan Balance	Principal Payment	Interest Payment	Total Annual Payment	Tax Savings	Net-Payment After Tax
1	$183,000	$0	$11,437	$11,437	$3,751	$7,686
2	$183,000	$0	$11,437	$11,437	$3,751	$7,686
3	$183,000	$0	$11,437	$11,437	$3,751	$7,686
4	$183,000	$0	$11,437	$11,437	$3,751	$7,686
5	$183,000	$0	$11,437	$11,437	$3,751	$7,686
6	$183,000	$0	$11,437	$11,437	$3,751	$7,686
7	$183,000	$0	$11,437	$11,437	$3,751	$7,686
8	$183,000	$0	$11,437	$11,437	$3,751	$7,686
9	$183,000	$0	$11,437	$11,437	$3,751	$7,686
10	$183,000	$0	$11,437	$11,437	$3,751	$7,686
11	$183,000	$0	$11,437	$11,437	$3,751	$7,686
12	$183,000	$0	$11,437	$11,437	$3,751	$7,686
13	$183,000	$0	$11,437	$11,437	$3,751	$7,686
14	$183,000	$0	$11,437	$11,437	$3,751	$7,686
15	$183,000	$0	$11,437	$11,437	$3,751	$7,686
16	$183,000	$0	$11,437	$11,437	$3,751	$7,686
17	$183,000	$0	$11,437	$11,437	$3,751	$7,686
18	$183,000	$0	$11,437	$11,437	$3,751	$7,686
19	$183,000	$0	$11,437	$11,437	$3,751	$7,686
20	$183,000	$0	$11,437	$11,437	$3,751	$7,686
21	$183,000	$0	$11,437	$11,437	$3,751	$7,686
22	$183,000	$0	$11,437	$11,437	$3,751	$7,686
23	$183,000	$0	$11,437	$11,437	$3,751	$7,686
24	$183,000	$0	$11,437	$11,437	$3,751	$7,686
25	$183,000	$0	$11,437	$11,437	$3,751	$7,686
26	$183,000	$0	$11,437	$11,437	$3,751	$7,686
27	$183,000	$0	$11,437	$11,437	$3,751	$7,686
28	$183,000	$0	$11,437	$11,437	$3,751	$7,686
29	$183,000	$0	$11,437	$11,437	$3,751	$7,686
30	$183,000	$0	$11,437	$11,437	$3,751	$7,686
TTL	$183,000	$0	$343,110	$343,110	$112,530	$230,580

(Figure 3.11 ~ Tax savings assume a state and federal marginal tax bracket of 32.8% multiplied by the interest payment. Net payment after tax equals the Total Payment less the Tax Savings.)

Year	Growth of $100,000 at Various Rates of Return		
	8%	6%	4%
1	$108,000.00	$106,000.00	$104,000.00
2	$116,640.00	$112,360.00	$108,160.00
3	$125,971.21	$119,101.60	$112,486.40
4	$136,048.90	$126,247.70	$116,985.86
5	$146,932.81	$133,822.56	$121,665.29
6	$158,687.43	$141,851.91	$126,531.90
7	$171,382.43	$150,363.03	$131,593.18
8	$185,093.02	$159,384.81	$136,856.91
9	$199,900.46	$168,947.90	$142,331.18
10	$215,892.50	$179,084.77	$148,024.43
11	$233,163.90	$189,829.86	$143,945.41
12	$251,817.01	$201,219.65	$160,103.22
13	$271,962.37	$213,292.83	$166,507.35
14	$293,719.36	$226,090.40	$173,167.64
15	$317,216.91	$239,655.82	$180,094.35
16	$342,594.26	$254,035.17	$187,298.12
17	$370,001.81	$269,277.28	$194,790.05
18	$399,601.95	$285,433.92	$202,581.65
19	$431,570.11	$302,559.95	$210,684.92
20	$466,095.71	$320,713.55	$219,112.31
21	$503,383.37	$339,956.36	$227,876.81
22	$543,654.04	$360,353.74	$236,991.88
23	$587,146.36	$381,974.97	$246,471.55
24	$634,118.07	$404,893.46	$256,330.42
25	$684,847.52	$429,187.07	$266,583.63
26	$739,635.32	$454,938.30	$277,246.98
27	$798,806.15	$482,234.59	$288,336.86
28	$862,710.64	$511,168.67	$299,870.33
29	$931,727.49	$541,838.79	$311,865.15
30	$1,006,265.69	$574,349.12	$324,339.75

(**Figure 3.12** ~ These examples do not represent any specific investment. No taxes or transactions costs have been taken into consideration. Investment vehicles will be discussed in chapter 7.)

This demonstrates the potential tax savings advantage of using the interest only loan. However, another advantage is the access to cash in the event of an emergency. If Jane is injured, losses her job, or has some other catastrophe and needs cash, she may not be able to remove her equity via a new mortgage loan. However, if she has already removed $100,000 of equity and she has it in an accessible place, she would be able to give herself time to get a job, get well, etc. before running out of money to meet her mortgage payment.

* * *

Two Caveats to the Interest Only Loan

Having demonstrated the dynamic wealth creation possible from utilizing an interest only loan and investing the difference in interest earning vehicles many people immediately wonder why one wouldn't simply refinance their home pulling out all of their equity and use all of it to realize huge profits while getting a tax write off on their mortgage interest. While every situation must be handled on a case by case basis, the Internal Revenue Code (IRC) gives us the rules on what may or may not be written off when it comes to mortgage interest. The IRC defines the rules and limits on the deductibility of mortgage interest as acquisitional indebtedness and home equity indebtedness.

Acquisitional indebtedness refers to some particular IRC rules regarding mortgage interest tax deductions. (As always, consult a tax professional regarding individual tax returns and questions of acquisitional indebtedness/home equity indebtedness) The cap on mortgage interest deductions for acquisitional indebtedness is $1,000,000. There are three basic steps in calculating one's acquisitional indebtedness. First, one determines how much debt was acquired to get into their real estate. Second, you must subtract how much you have paid down the original loan. Finally, you are allowed to add how much verifiable improvement has been made to the real estate. This final calculation is your acquisitional indebtedness.

Home equity indebtedness is another IRC regulation that basically states that you can write off the interest on an equity loan up to $100,000.

Again, these two regulations are the biggest reasons why most people who utilize any loan strategy (be they 30 year fixed loans, interest only loans or any variation of a mortgage loan) do not always get to write off the interest on their mortgage loans. Here's an example to illustrate. If you purchased your home for $500,000, and put $100,000 down at the time of purchase, have paid $50,000 of the principal down over the years, and have added $25,000 in verifiable home improvements, then your acquisitional indebtedness is $375,000 ($400,000 - $50,000 + $25,000 = $375,000). Home equity indebtedness means you can add another $100,000 in home equity indebtedness to that total for a grand total of $475,000. For this example you cannot take a mortgage interest tax deduction on any increased mortgage value above $475,000. The only way to increase this cap (up to the IRC maximum cap of $1,000,0000) would be to sell your home and purchase a new home at a higher value and incur a higher level of debt at purchase.

Many people have told us their stories of buying a house for $150,000 only to now have a mortgage in excess of both acquisitional and home equity indebtedness. They have been writing off their mortgage interest anyway because they never knew of the IRC rule regarding the deductibility of the same. This is an area that most loan officers, financial planners, and even CPA's are not aware of. It is our responsibility to tell you what the IRC says and recommend that you discuss your specific tax strategy with your tax and/or legal professional.

* * *

Summarizing the Better Mousetrap

Over the course of this chapter we have made numerous comparisons to results garnered through the use of fixed interest rate loans versus interest only loans. To briefly summarize, we want to reiterate that by considering an interest only loan one opens up the possibilities of:
1) earning interest on principal dollars
2) paying off one's loan early without increasing mortgage payments
3) reaping huge mortgage interest tax write offs
4) acquiring a sizeable investment gain that can be used to draw cash out throughout retirement and/or at time of personal need.

Because of the complex nature of proper equity management, Capital Republic Financial Group, Inc., under the leadership of the authors of this book, has developed a training course for mortgage & financial professionals to excel in the understanding and utilization of these concepts.

The Certified Mortgage Investment Advisor (CMIA) designation is granted to industry professionals that have completed the rigorous course, passed a comprehensive test, and agree to adhere to the Standards and Code of Ethics of the CMIA. Make sure the professional you are working with meets these minimum standards. Additional information regarding the CMIA can be found in the appendix.

To see if your advisor is a
Certified Mortgage Investment Advisor, visit
www.CMIADesignation.com

Chapter 4
Maximizing Cash Flow

Chapter 4
Maximizing Cash Flow

In the last chapter we made the case for why utilizing an interest only home loan can have tremendous wealth generation advantages over a traditional 30 year fixed interest loan. Not only are there incredible potential tax benefits, but the power of compound interest simply blows away the alternative of merely accruing equity in one's home. However, this is just the tip of the iceberg.

Most Americans have very little idea about the numerous products available in the area of home mortgages. In fact, the vast majority of Americans are under the assumption that the only distinction between mortgage products is the term of the loan (15 year or 30 year) and fixed or variable interest rates. Like so much of the conventional wisdom we've already addressed, this is far from the full picture.

In addition to the interest only loans that were addressed in the last chapter, another loan possibility is increasing in popularity among many Americans. It is known by several names, but most commonly it is referred to as an Option ARM loan.

* * *

Option ARM Loans and How They Work

An Option ARM loan is a mortgage product that attempts to provide the borrower with a wide array of financial flexibility, or options as the name implies. Most Option ARM loans provide the borrower with 4 payment options: 1) A 30 year payment (covering principal and interest), 2) A 15 year payment (covering principal and interest), 3) An interest only payment, and 4) A low monthly payment that defers interest (sometimes called "negative amortization"). One of the basic advantages of this type of loan is the payment flexibility it affords the borrower. Each month the borrower chooses which of the four payment options that best suit their current financial needs and then makes their payment accordingly. In the case of the first two options (15 year and 30 year payment) the loan operates like any other 15 or 30 year ARM loan. The payment is amortized and, if chosen every time a payment is due, will pay the loan off in the prescribed 15 or 30 year term. The third option (interest only) was covered last chapter and the advantages mentioned still apply to the interest only loan as a part of an Option ARM loan. The fourth option (low monthly payment, sometimes also called the "minimum payment") gives the borrower the option to pay an amount lower, and often significantly lower, than the interest only payment. Additionally, this minimum payment usually has a low starting interest rate, often as low as 1% or 2%. It is this payment flexibility that tends to first attract people to the Option ARM loan.

* * *

Payment Flexibility as a Means of Security

The minimum payment option in the Option ARM loan is a very attractive feature to many home buyers. The "safety net" factor of realizing that a low monthly payment can be made in lieu of the amortized 30 year or 15 year payment is a comforting reassurance to many home owners. In fact, I've seen this product come to the rescue of clients in the past. The story of the Maxwells comes to mind and will illustrate the point.

A couple of years ago John and Kathy Maxwell were determined to adhere to the conventional wisdom regarding their acquisition of a home loan. They had been taught that the only decision to be considered was whether to get a 15 year or a 30 year loan. With fixed rates being low, that also seemed to them the only way to go. Fortunately, as their future would prove, they were open to other possible loan products.

The Maxwells came to me and asked my opinion about their decision to get a 15 year fixed rate mortgage. Their thinking was that this would lock in the lowest fixed interest rate available and guarantee that their mortgage would be paid off in a much shorter period than most people pay off their homes. I told them that their thinking was sound, as long as everything went according to plan. They asked, "With a fixed payment and loan term, what could be outside the plan?" I tactfully broached the subject of personal injury or illness. We discussed the possibility of having children in the future which could result in Kathy leaving the workforce. We talked over the possibility of downsizing or job loss. We discussed several more possible scenarios regarding their future as it related to their income and their ability to make their fixed monthly mortgage payment. The more we discussed, the more the uncertainty of the future became clear.

It was at this point that I explained to the Maxwells about Option ARM loans. I thought that the four payment options would fit perfectly with their loan needs. On the one hand, if everything went according to their plan, they could exercise the 15 year full payment option and own their home free and clear in 15 years. However, if the unexpected happened, the Maxwells would have the flexibility of paying the interest only payment or even the minimum payment to stay afloat. The Option ARM loan would allow the Maxwells to have their cake (fixed term payments to complete their loan if everything went according to plan) and eat it too (flexible lower payments in the event of financial hardship). The Maxwells started the paperwork for an Option ARM loan that same day. In hindsight, it was a choice that quite possibly saved their home.

    A few months later, the Maxwells were paying the 15 year monthly payment and heading steadily towards their goal of owning their home free and clear in a relatively short amount of time. However, out of nowhere, John got downsized and was looking for work. Fortunately, Kathy was still working so they continued to have an income stream, although things were now tight with the loss of John's job. Unfortunately, Kathy also lost her job just a short time after John lost his. Fortunately, as finances grew thin, the Maxwells were able to exercise the minimum monthly payment option on their Option ARM loan. It set them back a few years in terms of paying off their loan in 15 years, but the alternative of missed payments, damaged credit scores, and potential foreclosure on their home made this an easy choice.

    The good news is that the Maxwells both eventually found new jobs and were able to ultimately get back to making the full 15 year payments. They are now well on their way to achieving their goal of owning their home free and clear. However, the American dream of home ownership could have easily become an unbearable nightmare, possibly resulting in the loss of their home, if not for the flexibility of payments that the Option ARM loan provided the Maxwells.

***
The Mechanics of an Option ARM Loan

There is no denying that the most obvious feature that attracts Americans to Option ARM loans is the payment flexibility. However, while the minimum monthly payment option can be used to provide leverage in times of financial difficulty (such as The Maxwell's story illustrates), the minimum monthly payment option can also be used as a potential cash flow maximizing tool.

Much like we demonstrated in the previous chapter the tremendous wealth generating potential of utilizing an interest only loan versus a fixed amortized payment loan, there is even greater wealth generating potential utilizing the minimum payment option of an Option ARM loan versus a fixed amortized payment. However, before we discuss the specifics of the wealth generating strategies that can be used with an Option ARM loan, we should examine the basic mechanics of the Option ARM loan. The two key mechanics that need to be understood are 1) How the variable interest rate is calculated and 2) the loan recast point.

An Option ARM loan works quite similarly to traditional fixed payment loans. The borrower acquires the loan and then begins the process of paying back the original loan amount plus interest over time. An Option ARM loan, being an adjustable interest rate product, determines its current interest rate by determining the current interest rate of the financial index it is tied to (COFI, COSI, MTA, etc.). Which one of the financial indices the individual loan is tied to is determined during the generation of the loan. Once the index is determined, the margin is added to the rate to establish the actual current interest rate of the loan. The margin is the percentage added to the index rate which is pre-determined at the generation of the loan. The margin, unlike the index, does not fluctuate. It is a fixed amount that is always added to the index to determine the actual current interest rate of the loan. Let us use an example of a couple (we'll call them Stan and Martha) and how the loan mechanics would work in acquiring an Option ARM loan.

Stan and Martha decide to acquire an Option ARM loan. In their loan documents it states that their particular loan will be tied to the COFI index. Therefore, to determine how much their loan's variable rate will be to start, we first need to find out what the current COFI index is at. Additionally, the margin agreed to in their loan is 2.85%. Therefore their variable rate will always be whatever the rate of the COFI index is plus the 2.85% margin. While the numbers vary, the formula remains constant. To determine the current actual variable interest rate on the loan they will always use the following formula: Index Rate + Margin = Current Actual Interest Rate (often referred to as the Fully Indexed Rate).

The big difference between an Option ARM loan and a traditional loan is called the recast point. The recast point of an Option ARM loan comes into play either at a fixed point in the loan (usually five years) or when the borrower chooses to exercise the minimum monthly payment option. The minimum monthly payment option is an amount below the interest only payment which means that the minimum monthly payment not only applies none of the payment towards the reduction of the loan principal, it also is insufficient to cover the entirety of the interest portion of the payment. The result of making the minimum monthly payment is that interest that is not being paid is deferred to the loan principal (also sometimes referred to as negative amortization). This ultimately means that if the minimum payment option was continuously exercised, the principal loan balance would be consistently increasing. Lenders do not want loans growing to 50% or 100% larger than their original value. To prevent excessive growth above the original loan amount, the recast point comes into play. The recast point is a percentage, determined at the origination of the loan, above the original loan amount that the lender will allow the borrower to incur. However, once this percentage is attained (usually 10%, 15%, or 25% above the original loan amount), the loan is then recast as an amortized loan. The interest only and minimum payment options become unavailable and the loan (the original amount + the deferred interest) must now be paid off in amortized payments over the remaining term of the loan.

To illustrate, our friends Stan and Martha, who acquired the Option ARM loan in our previous example, decide to exercise the minimum monthly payment option of their Option ARM loan. Let's say the original loan amount is $400,000. The minimum payment on this loan (assuming a minimum payment start rate of 1.25%) would be $1,333. However, the interest only payment (assuming a fully indexed rate of 7%) would be $2,333. This means that $1,000 would accrue monthly as deferred interest. In other words, at the end of the first month of Stan and Martha's loan they would owe $401,000 (the original $400,000 loan principal + $1,000, which was the difference between the interest only payment and the minimum monthly payment, = $401,000). If Stan and Martha continued to pay only the minimum monthly payment eventually they will have added thousands of dollars to the original loan and, depending on how long they exercise the minimum payment they may even exceed the original value of the loan! To prevent this from happening, mortgage lenders insert a recast point into the original loan agreement. For sake of illustration, we'll assume that Stan and Martha's recast point was set at 125% of the original loan value (recast points vary between 110-125% typically of the original loan balance). This means that Stan and Martha would be able to defer interest up to a loan amount of $500,000 (100% of the original loan value which was $400,000 + 25% of the original loan value which is $100,000 = 125% recast point which is $500,000). Once Stan and Martha reach the recast point the lender is basically saying that the size of the loan is getting too large. Therefore, the borrowers must stop adding to the amount of the loan and begin paying down the loan.

* * *

Minimum Payment to Maximize Cash Flow

With an understanding of the basic mechanics of an Option ARM loan under our belt, it's time to examine some strategies that allow us to use an Option ARM loan for tremendous potential wealth generation.

The key to wealth generation utilizing an Option ARM loan lies with the minimum monthly payment option. At its most basic level, this strategy is similar to the one outlined in the previous chapter that analyzed the cash flow difference between paying down ones mortgage using a fixed rate loan and accruing equity versus making an interest only payment and saving the difference in another investment vehicle. As the numbers presented indicated, the difference can be staggering. However, the same strategy can be utilized using the Option ARM loan with even greater potential results. Let us return to our example of Stan and Martha to demonstrate the way wealth can be generated using the minimum monthly payment of an Option ARM loan.

To refresh our memories, Stan and Martha acquired an Option ARM loan for $400,000. Their loan is tied to the COFI index which we'll assume is at 4.150%. Their margin is 2.850%. All together their current actual interest rate on their loan is 7.0%. They have the flexibility to choose from four payment options. If they choose the traditional 30 year payment they will have to pay $2,661 per month, at the current interest rate, for 30 years to pay off their loan. If they choose the 15 year payment they will have to pay $3,595 per month, at the current interest rate, for 15 years to pay off their loan. Stan and Martha also have the option to make the interest only payment. At the current interest rate their interest only payment would be $2,333. This payment would save Stan and Martha $328 per month versus making the traditional 30 year payment. However, this does nothing to reduce the loan principal. The final option available to Stan and Martha is the minimum payment option. At a start rate of 1.25% their monthly payment would be $1,333. This amounts to a whopping $1,328 savings every month over the traditional 30 year payment. Even more impressive, this amounts to a $15,938 savings after the first year of payments. It is this savings difference that has the potential to generate tremendous wealth. (Figure 4.1)

Just like in the previous chapter with the interest only loan, the key to wealth generation is not paying down principal and acquiring equity that earns no interest. The key, rather, is in using the power of compound interest to grow your money. In the previous chapter we illustrated the point by showing the wealth accumulation possible by saving the difference between the 30 year payment and the interest only payment for 30 years. To demonstrate the

Stan & Martha				Term (months)		360	
Home Value	$500,000			Min Pay Rate		1.25%	
Untapped Equity	$100,000	20%					
				Fully Indexed Rate:		7.000%	
Option ARM Amt:	$400,000	80%		Margin:		2.850%	
				Index:		4.150%	
				Recast Percent		125%	

YEAR	Low Minimum Payment	Interest Only Payment	Traditional 30 Year Payment	15 Year Payment	Monthly Cash Flow	Annual Cash Flow	Monthly Deferred Interest
1	$1,333.01	$2,333.33	$2,661.21	$3,595.31	$1,328.20	$15,938.44	$1,000.33

Annual Deferred Interest	New House Value at 3% growth	New House Value at 5% growth
$12,003.92	$515,000.00	$525,000.00

(*Figure 4.1* ~ This is a hypothetical example to illustrate the cash flow difference between the fully indexed rate and the minimum payment. There is no guarantee that the Index used will remain the same month after month. Therefore the deferred interest may be higher or lower than the illustration.)

powerful potential of the Option ARM minimum monthly payment to generate wealth, let us present an example that only requires saving the difference between the traditional 30 year payment and the minimum monthly payment for five years.

Stan and Martha decide to pay the minimum monthly payment of $1,333. The savings (the difference between the traditional 30 year monthly payment of $2,661 and the minimum monthly payment of $1,333) they decide to invest for the next five years. An important point to understand with this loan is that the minimum payment will increase each year. Most Option ARM loans are set up so that the maximum the minimum payment can increase each year is 7.5% of the previous year's minimum payment. This is the minimum payment we are talking about, not the interest rate. Assuming the maximum payment increase by contract (7.5% per year) their monthly savings would be as follows:

Month 1-12: $1,333   Year 1 total: $15,938
Month 13-24: $1,433   Year 2 total: $14,739
Month 25-36: $1,540   Year 3 total: $13,449
Month 37-48: $1,656   Year 4 total: $12,063
Month 49-60: $1,780   Year 5 total: $10,572
                             Grand Total: $66,761

(Figure 4.2)

The only thing left to do at this point is calculate the rate of interest that the savings will grow at. Let's plug in some numbers.

Assuming a 6% rate of return, the first year savings would grow to $16,466.01 ($1,328.20 x 12 @ 6% interest). The second year would grow to $32,708.26. The third year would grow to $48,619.85. The fourth year would grow to $64,080.57. Finally, the fifth year would grow to $78,955.13.

At this point the loan would recast (most Option ARM loans are designed to recast at the 5th year). This means no more minimum payments, rather, the loan amortizes for the remainder of the loan term. In this case, the loan amortizes as a 25 year loan (original loan term of 30 years − 5 years of minimum monthly payments = 25 years remaining on the loan term). So, over the next 25 years the loan balance is slowly being paid off and no more new money is being added to the savings. However, the existing money continues to earn interest. This is where the compounding effect really pays off. Over the next 5 years of the loan (years 6-10 of the loan term) the $78,955.13 we left off with will have no more new money added to it. However, at 6% interest it will grow to $106,498.64. This compounding will occur every year. At the end of the next 5

78 - The New Mortgage Investment Advisor

Stan & Martha				Term (months)		360
Home Value	$500,000			Min Pay Rate		1.25%
Untapped Equity	$100,000	20%				
				Fully Indexed Rate:		7.000%
Option ARM Amt	$400,000	80%		Margin:		2.850%
				Index:		4.150%
				Recast Percent		125%

YEAR	Low Minimum Payment	Interest Only Payment	Traditional 30 Year Payment	15 Year Payment	Monthly Cash Flow	Annual Cash Flow	Monthly Deferred Interest
1	$1,333.01	$2,333.33	$2,661.21	$3,595.31	$1,328.20	$15,938.44	$1,000.3:
2	$1,432.98	$2,333.33	$2,661.21	$3,595.31	$1,228.23	$14,738.73	$900.35
3	$1,540.46	$2,333.33	$2,661.21	$3,595.31	$1,120.75	$13,449.05	$792.88
4	$1,655.99	$2,333.33	$2,661.21	$3,595.31	$1,005.22	$12,062.64	$677.34
5	$1,780.19	$2,333.33	$2,661.21	$3,595.31	$881.02	$10,572.25	$553.14

Annual Deferred Interest	New Principal Balance on Loan	New House Value at 3% growth	New House Value at 5% growth
$12,003.92	$412,003.92	$515,000.00	$525,000.00
$10,804.21	$422,808.13	$530,450.00	$551,250.00
$9,514.53	$432,322.66	$546,363.50	$578,812.50
$8,128.12	$440,450.78	$562,754.41	$607,753.13
$6,637.73	$447,088.51	$579,637.04	$638,140.78

(*Figure 4.2* ~ This is a hypothetical example to illustrate the cash flow difference between the fully indexed rate and the minimum payment. There is no guarantee that the Index used will remain the same month after month. Therefore the deferred interest may be higher or lower than the illustration.)

years (years 11-15 of the loan term) the savings will grow to $143,650.71. The next 5 years (years 16-20 of the loan term) the savings will grow to $193,763.28. The next 5 years (years 21-25 of the loan term) the savings will grow to $261,357.63. At the completion of the loan (year 30) the savings will have grown to $352,532.27. This is almost the amount of the original $400,000 loan! Additionally, all of this wealth was compiled through only adding new money during the first 5 years. Further, since the loan amortized into a 25 year loan,

Maximizing Cash Flow - 79

Assumed Interest Rate:	4%, 6%, 8%
Total Cash Flow Savings:	$66,761.04

Year	Monthly Cash Flow Savings on New Loan	Hypothetical Growth at 4.0%	Hypothetical Growth at 6.0%	Hypothetical Growth at 8.0%
1	$1,328.20	$16,287.99	$16,466.01	$16,646.23
2	$1,228.23	$32,013.62	$32,708.26	$33,421.18
3	$1,120.75	$47,061.89	$48,619.85	$50,241.39
4	$1,005.22	$61,306.48	$64,080.57	$67,009.75
5	$881.02	$74,608.33	$78,955.13	$83,613.29
6		$77,647.99	$83,824.91	$90,553.15
7		$80,811.49	$88,995.05	$98,069.01
8		$84,103.88	$94,484.07	$106,208.69
9		$87,530.40	$100,311.64	$115,023.96
10		$91,096.52	$106,498.64	$124,570.90
11		$94,807.93	$113,067.24	$134,910.22
12		$98,670.56	$120,040.98	$146,107.70
13		$102,690.55	$127,444.85	$158,234.57
14		$106,874.32	$135,305.37	$171,367.96
15		$111,228.54	$143,650.71	$185,591.41
16		$115,760.16	$152,510.77	$200,995.41
17		$120,476.41	$161,917.30	$217,677.93
18		$125,384.81	$171,904.00	$235,745.09
19		$130,493.18	$182,506.67	$255,311.82
20		$135,809.67	$193,763.28	$276,502.57
21		$141,342.77	$205,714.17	$299,452.15
22		$147,101.29	$218,402.17	$324,306.53
23		$153,094.42	$231,872.74	$351,223.81
24		$159,331.73	$246,174.14	$380,375.21
25		$165,823.15	$261,357.63	$411,946.17
26		$172,579.04	$277,477.59	$446,137.50
27		$179,610.17	$294,591.80	$483,166.69
28		$186,927.77	$312,761.58	$523,269.29
29		$194,543.49	$332,052.03	$566,700.38
30		$202,469.50	$352,532.27	$613,736.23

(*Figure 4.3* ~ Growth of the savings compounding monthly at 4, 6, & 8% generated during the first 5 years by the difference between the minimum payment and the 30 year payment.)

the mortgage would be paid in full. This $352,532.27 would be in addition to owning the house free and clear. (Figure 4.3)

Obviously, the final results will vary depending on the interest rate the savings compounds at. Just as a quick comparison, the same savings strategy earning 8% interest grows to $83,613.37 by the end of the fifth year. As it compounds over time, at the end of the 30 year loan term, the savings would have grown to $613,736.23! This is over $200,000 above the original loan amount of $400,000!

Some skeptics argue that an 8% rate of return is wishful thinking. While we would beg to differ, the point of tremendous potential wealth generation can still be easily made using a 4% interest example. Using the exact same savings strategy and substituting a savings interest rate of 4% instead of 8%, the results are still impressive. At the end of the first 5 years where new money is being added by saving the difference between the 30 year payment and the minimum monthly payment the total savings would amount to $74,608.41. As this process of interest compounding and no new money being added continues over the course of the 30 year loan term, the final savings amount would be a healthy $202,469.70.

The potential wealth generation of this strategy should be obvious. However, keep in mind that the examples provided assume only 5 years of adding new money. The increase in wealth grows significantly if new money is put in for just a few more years, let alone the astounding difference if new money is continuously added to the savings (such as redoing the Option ARM loan every 3-5 years to start the savings process again). However, regardless of the time period chose to add new money, people are missing out on a huge opportunity to generate wealth by simply paying down their traditional mortgages instead of saving the difference in some type of interest earning account.

* * *
How It Can Go Wrong!

Clearly we believe in these powerful wealth generating strategies and are excited by the huge financial rewards that can be realized by people who will question the conventional wisdom and change the way they look at paying their mortgage. However, we are also aware of the negative image some hold towards Option ARM loans. We are also aware of many people who have had horrible experiences trying to use Option ARM loans. While there are certain risks, we believe the negative image of Option ARM loans and the stories of woe some associate with them can be summarized by the old adage used to explain why some people failed in the 12 step program made famous by Alcoholics Anonymous, **"It's not that the program doesn't work, it's that you failed to work the program."** This maxim applies frequently to borrowers that acquire Option ARM loans and fall into trouble. Having said that, let us address the most common arguments against using Option ARM loans and examine the ways in which using Option ARM loans can go wrong.

The two most common arguments given against Option ARM loans are as follows:

Argument #1- "Using the minimum monthly payment defers interest which adds to the principal balance. How can any money be truly saved if the principal is increasing?"

Answer- It is true that using the minimum monthly payment defers interest which adds to the principal balance. However, keep in mind (as explained in previous chapters) the difference between compounding and amortizing. If $100,000 is amortized as a 30 year payment at 8% interest, the result is $264,155.25 paid (the original $100,000 loan amount + 30 years of amortized interest). On the other hand, $100,000 compounding over 30 years (and assuming interest is only compounded 1 time annually) at 8% interest amounts to $1,006,265.69! Even at 4% interest, after 30 years of compounding the $100,000 would grow to $324,339.75. That's a $67,194.55 difference and it happened earning half the savings rate of the amortized loan interest rate! The point is that saving versus paying down, even when taking on more debt, creates far greater wealth. (Figure 4.4)

$100,000 Loan
8% Interest Rate

~ ~ ~ ~ ~

Monthly Payment of $733.76
$733.76 x 360 months (30 years)
Over 30 years the payback is:

$264,155.25

$100,000 Investment
8% Growth Rate
(Compounded Annually)

~ ~ ~ ~ ~ ~

$1,006,265.69

$100,000 Investment
6% Growth Rate
(Compounded Annually)

~ ~ ~ ~ ~ ~

$574,349.12

$100,000 Investment
4% Growth Rate
(Compounded Annually)

~ ~ ~ ~ ~ ~

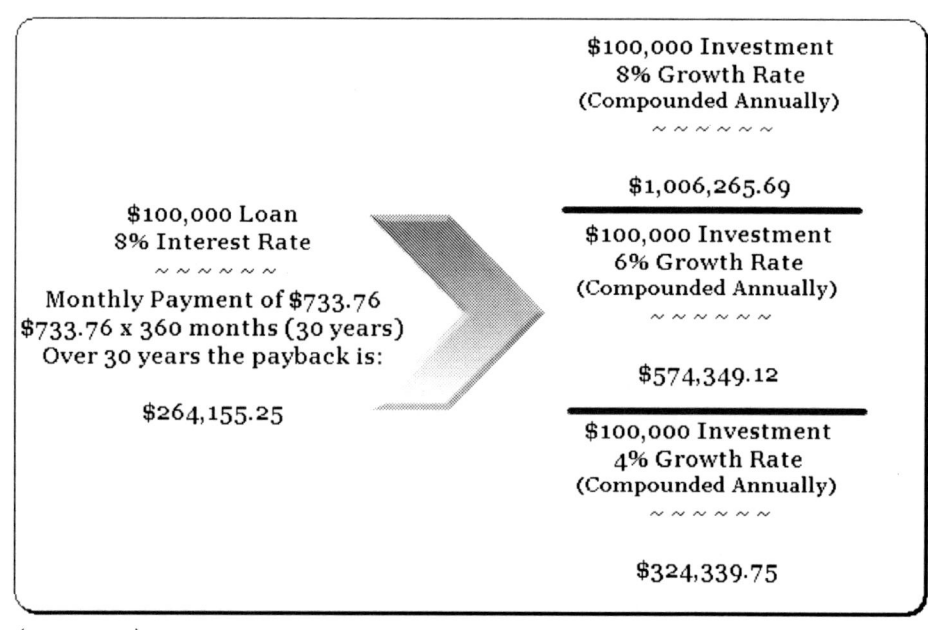

$324,339.75

(Figure 4.4)

Another relevant point is to remind the objectors of the recast point. It is not possible to defer interest to the point where the loan principal is doubled. Again, most Option ARM loans have a recast point between 110% and 125%. This puts the brakes on people from acquiring too much extra principal.

Argument #2- "I know people that got an Option ARM loan for their loan needs. However, once the recast point came in to play, they were required to pay almost double their minimum monthly payment in order to meet the new amortized monthly payment amount. As a result, they could not afford the new payment and they lost their house! Why would anyone choose an Option ARM and have this possibly happen to them?"

Answer- Stories like this are, sadly, all too common. However, blaming the situation on the Option ARM loan is the equivalent of blaming swimming pools for drowning deaths. Swimming pools do not reach out and drag people under. Unfortunately, some people who cannot swim put themselves in the pool with tragic consequences. The same can be said regarding some people and their choosing Option ARM loans.

An Option ARM loan should never be chosen if the full 30 year payment cannot be made. Purchasing a house where one can only make the minimum payment means that too much house has been purchased when considering that person's income level. The Option ARM loan is a product that provides flexibility, but it cannot perform magic. A person who cannot make the full 30 year payment and took an Option ARM loan to afford a more expensive house using the minimum monthly payment has made a terrible financial decision. However, again, millions of people swim in their pools safely and love the experience. Much like a pool is a tool, that when used properly and in the right conditions, results in rewards for the swimmer, an Option ARM loan is a tool, that when used properly and in the right conditions, can result in flexibility and potential financial reward for the borrower.

* * *

In addition to these common arguments, a few more warnings should cover almost all objections to an Option ARM loan.

How It Can Go Wrong Warning #1- Too low of a start rate with an increasing variable interest rate can lead to an early recast point.

While all of us have been trained to search for the lowest interest rate, it is possible that too low of a starting interest rate could lead to an early recast. Some Option ARM loans offer low starting rates for their minimum monthly payment option below 1%. While this is incredible in terms of an interest rate, it means that more deferred interest would be accrued faster. Once the deferred interest reaches the recast point, the minimum monthly payment is taken away as an option. The warning for the borrower is simply to be aware that the recast point can arrive sooner in the loan term than originally forecast. However, the risk is minimal at most if one maintains an awareness of how much interest they are deferring and if they can afford the 30 year traditional payment anyway (as we've already addressed).

How It Can Go Wrong Warning #2- Not saving the difference between the minimum monthly payment and the traditional 30 year payment can lead to financial disaster.

The only way that wealth can be generated using the minimum monthly payment is to save the difference. Too many people run into trouble because they don't save the difference, rather, they spend the difference. Not only then does no wealth get generated in this situation, but deferred interest is being added to the loan principal. **This is the recipe for disaster that many hear about from friends or in the media when dealing with Option ARM loans.** Again, the problem isn't a faulty loan product. The problem is undisciplined people who use the product foolishly. The simple warning is that you must save the difference, not spend it!

How It Can Go Wrong Warning #3- Taking money out of savings kills your assets

People who do save the difference, but withdraw funds from their savings destroy the growth of their savings. In order for the strategy to work, one must not only save the difference between the minimum monthly payment and the traditional 30 year payment, they must allow the savings to compound over time. Each withdrawal lowers the amount of savings earning interest. Even small withdrawals can have a huge impact on the final amount saved with interest compounding. For maximum growth, do not withdraw from your savings. Allow it to compound over time.

* * *

While slightly more sophisticated than a basic interest only loan, the strategy for wealth generation using an Option ARM loan is basically the same. Investing the difference between the minimum monthly payment and the traditional 30 year payment affords borrowers a tremendous opportunity to grow their personal wealth.

The only real glaring risk that hasn't been addressed regarding the Option ARM loan is the potential for the variable interest rate to continuously increase during the life of the loan. Up until recently this was simply a risk one had to be willing to take in order to utilize the Option ARM loan for wealth generation. Fortunately, much of that risk has been eliminated with the creation of a new loan product. We will discuss this product in detail in the next chapter.

Because of the complex nature of proper equity management, Capital Republic Financial Group, Inc., under the leadership of the authors of this book, has developed a training course for mortgage & financial professionals to excel in the understanding and utilization of these concepts.

The Certified Mortgage Investment Advisor (CMIA) designation is granted to industry professionals that have completed the rigorous course, passed a comprehensive test, and agree to adhere to the Standards and Code of Ethics of the CMIA. Make sure the professional you are working with meets these minimum standards. Additional information regarding the CMIA can be found in the appendix.

To see if your advisor is a
Certified Mortgage Investment Advisor, visit
www.CMIADesignation.com

Chapter 5
Maximizing Cash Flow, Minimizing Risks

Chapter 5
Maximizing Cash Flow, Minimizing Risks

As more and more Americans discovered the potential for wealth generation through saving the difference between the minimum monthly payment and the traditional 30 year payment, lenders began exploring ways to make the Option ARM loan more attractive to potential clients. Over and over lenders were told that the biggest factor that steered borrowers away from an Option ARM loan was the variable interest rate and how its fluctuations could not only lead to an early loan recast point, but could make the amortized payment after the loan recast unaffordable. These issues and more have been addressed by the arrival of a new product on the lending scene. This new product is known as a Secured Option ARM loan (sometimes called the Hybrid Option ARM).

As the name implies, this new loan focuses on minimizing the risks inherent in a traditional Option ARM loan while still providing the financial flexibility that make traditional Option ARM loans so attractive. Let's examine how the Secured Option ARM loan works.

* * *

Mechanics of a Secured Option ARM Loan

In many ways a Secured Option ARM loan works like a traditional Option ARM loan. This is most apparent regarding the payment options. Just like the traditional Option ARM loan, a Secured Option ARM loan has four payment options: 1) a traditional 30 year payment, 2) a 15 year payment, 3) an interest only payment, and 4) a minimum monthly payment. This gives the Secured Option ARM loan the exact same flexibility as the traditional Option ARM loan.

Also like the traditional Option ARM loan, the Secured Option ARM has a recast point to prevent an excess of deferred interest for those who choose to exercise the minimum monthly payment option. The recast point for Secured Option ARM loans is typically set at 115% of the original loan value or at the end of year 5 of the loan, whichever comes first.

These are the two main similarities between the Secured Option ARM loan and the traditional Option ARM loan. Obviously there are differences. However, it is these differences that give the Secured Option ARM loan its advantages over traditional Option ARM loans.

* * *

Difference #1- How the Minimum Monthly Payment is Calculated

The first difference between the two loans is how they calculate and determine the interest rate of the minimum monthly payment. To refresh our memories, in the previous chapter we learned that the interest rate for an Option ARM loan is calculated by determining what the current interest rate is of the index that the loan is tied to (COSI, COFI, MTA, etc.) Then, the margin is added to the index rate to determine the actual interest rate for the loan. This process of determining the actual interest rate is the same for both the Secured Option ARM loan and the traditional Option ARM loan.

At this point, both loans would determine what the minimum monthly payment rate would be. For traditional Option ARM loans, a low starting rate is basically chosen. 1% or 2% are the common rates picked because they represent low rates in the minds of many consumers. The Secured Option ARM loan, on the other hand determines its minimum monthly interest rate using a simple formula. The Secured Option ARM loan takes the actual interest rate and subtracts 3 points to determine the minimum monthly interest rate (some lenders have subtle differences in how they calculate the minimum payment rate, but we will use this). This means, for example, if the fully indexed interest rate for a Secured Option ARM loan was 7%, the interest on the minimum monthly payment would be 4% (7% actual interest rate − 3 points = 4% minimum monthly payment interest rate).

This is the basic difference between how the two loans determine the interest rate for the minimum monthly payment. Many people see the difference as simply a procedural difference, or worse, as merely trivial. However, it is this difference in calculation that gives the Secured Option ARM loan one of its greatest advantages over traditional Option ARM loans. Let us attempt to explain.

The Secured Option ARM minimum monthly interest rate is a fixed rate which constitutes an interest only payment. The traditional Option ARM loan, on the other hand, is calculated as if it were a principal and interest payment on a 30 year loan. Let us provide an illustration for clarity.

Dick and Jane are shopping for a $400,000 home loan. They understand that they can generate a tremendous amount of wealth if they go against the conventional wisdom of purchasing a 30 year fixed rate loan. The big decision they are deliberating over is whether to acquire a traditional Option ARM loan or a Secured Option ARM loan. They first look at the numbers for the traditional Option ARM loan. They examine a loan tied to the 12MTA index which, for the sake of example, is at 4.150%. The margin on this loan is 2.85% which means the actual interest for the loan is 7.0%. The loan is offering a minimum monthly payment with a 1.25% starting interest rate. To determine the minimum monthly payment for this loan one must calculate the amortized payments for principal and interest on $400,000 at 1.25% interest. In this case, the monthly payment amount is $1,333 a month for the minimum monthly payment.

Dick and Jane then take a look at the Secured Option ARM loan offerings. They find one also tied to the 12MTA index, which means that the index would be the same as the traditional Option ARM loan. The margin for this loan is 2.85% (in reality, these two loans would not have the same margin available but for the sake of this example we are going to compare these loans as if they did) which puts the actual interest rate for this loan at 7.0%. The minimum monthly payment is calculated by taking the actual interest rate and subtracting 3 points. In this example the interest rate for the minimum monthly payment would be 4% (7% actual interest rate - 3 points = 4% interest on the minimum monthly payment).

At this point, Dick and Jane (and most other Americans as well) think the choice is clear. At 1.25% interest, the traditional Option ARM is 2.75% lower than the Secured Option ARM loan. People's natural financial intuition is that the traditional Option ARM is the way to go. However, if these people would ignore their intuition for a moment and finish calculating the payment they would be amazed at how off their intuition was.

Remember, the minimum monthly payment on a Secured Option ARM loan is calculated as an interest only payment. To calculate an interest only payment one takes the amount of the loan multiplied by the interest rate. This total is the yearly payment amount. Since mortgage loans are typically paid monthly, divide the yearly total by 12 to get the monthly amount. So, to calculate the minimum monthly payment for the Secured Option ARM loan using the Dick and Jane example above, you simply plug our numbers into the steps set forth above: 1) original loan amount ($400,000) x interest rate (4%) = $16,000. $16,000 is the annual amount to be paid if one chooses the minimum monthly payment on the Secured Option ARM loan. To figure out how much that is monthly one simply divides $16,000 by 12. The result is $1,333! This is the exact same monthly payment amount as the traditional Option ARM loan.

Most people, at this point, assume there has been some sort of mathematical mistake made. How can a loan with a 1.25% interest rate have the same monthly payment as a loan with a 4% interest rate? There has been no mistake made. Remember, each loan calculates the payment differently. The traditional Option ARM loan, despite its lower interest rate, calculates the minimum monthly payment as a principal and interest payment on a 30 year loan. The Secured Option ARM loan calculates the minimum monthly payment as an interest only payment. This difference in calculation is what allows two loans with differing interest rates to have, using the numbers in our example, identical payments.

Hopefully the mechanics of how each loan calculates their minimum monthly payment is clear. The important factor to grasp is that the interest rate is not the only consideration to make. A lower starting rate does not guarantee a lower payment. You must determine how the payment is calculated to determine which loan is the better value.

* * *

Difference #2- Fixed Rate and Payment

A second difference between the traditional Option ARM loan and the Secured Option ARM loan is that the Secured Option ARM has a fixed interest rate and payment for the first five years of the loan. The traditional Option ARM loan has a variable rate which adjusts monthly, beginning typically after the first month of the loan. This can amount to a big difference in monthly payments. Let us return to our example with Dick and Jane to examine the numbers.

If Dick and Jane choose the traditional Option ARM loan, the minimum monthly payment on a $400,000 loan at 1.25% interest is $1,333. However, since this interest rate is variable it adjusts every month. This means that if rates rise, then the amount of deferred interest (or negative amortization) that one is adding to the principal of the loan will increase above the amount expected when the loan was started. However, if rates decrease, then the amount of negative amortization that one expected would decrease. Also, the minimum payment will increase every year by a maximum of 7.5% of the previous year's payment.

There are two disadvantages for the borrower in this scenario. The first, and more glaring, disadvantage is that the payment is increasing. The difference between the 1st year minimum monthly payment and the 5th year minimum monthly payment is $447.18. That's up to $447.18 each month that is not going towards growing wealth. The second, and not nearly as apparent, disadvantage is that as the interest rates increase, the amount of deferred interest increases as well. This can cause the loan to recast early. Not only can this be unpleasant because it catches some people by surprise, it is also unpleasant because this loan recasts into a variable rate loan. At this point this could be potentially problematic because the interest rates were increasing (the reason the loan recast early in the first place) and now the borrower would be stuck with a variable rate amortized loan that could adjust upwards on a monthly basis.

The Secured Option ARM loan avoids these downsides associated with the traditional Option ARM loan in this example. Let us return to Dick and Jane one more time.

If Dick and Jane take the Secured Option ARM loan their monthly payment (at 4% interest only as the minimum payment) would be $1,333. Since the 4% is a fixed rate for 5 years, Dick and Jane know with confidence how much deferred interest (or negative amortization) will be added to the loan. This is advantageous to Dick and Jane for two reasons. First, the psychological comfort of knowing their payment is fixed for 5 years is hard to put a price on. Needless to say most people love the comfort of feeling in control. Second, since the payment is fixed, one can potentially grow more wealth as compared to the fluctuating payment associated with the traditional Option ARM loan. Remember that since the traditional Option ARM loan uses a variable interest rate it can cause the 30 year and 15 year payments to fluctuate monthly. Further, if interest rates continuously rise, then the amount of deferred interest increases which means a higher payment at the time of recast..

* * *

Further Advantages of the Secured Option ARM Loan

The next advantage the Secured Option ARM loan has over the traditional Option ARM loan comes at the recast point of the loan. With the traditional Option ARM loan, at the recast point, the loan converts into an amortized loan. This means no more minimum monthly payments and no more interest only payments. At this point an amortized payment would be made for the remainder of the life of the loan. In contrast, the Secured Option ARM loan, at the recast point, becomes an interest only loan until year 10 (for most Secured Option ARMs). Let us return to Dick and Jane to illustrate.

If Dick and Jane were using a traditional Option ARM loan, at the recast point their ability to utilize the minimum monthly payment and the interest only payment options would be gone. Further, the loan would now be recast as an amortized payment loan for the remainder of the loan term. This would have a huge effect on the monthly payments. Using the loan calculations from the previous examples and assuming the loan recast at year 5 (and the interest rate remained at 7.0% for the entire time) the monthly payment would jump from $1,780 per month to $3,160 per month. This new payment is an amortized monthly payment based on a loan balance of $447,088.51 (the original $400,000 loan + $47,088.51 in deferred interest accrued over the past 5 years) at the fully indexed rate (not the minimum monthly rate

Dick and Jane had grown accustomed to) of 7.0% interest amortized over 25 years (the original loan term of 30 years – 5 years of minimum monthly payments = 25 years of amortized payments remaining in the loan term). This loan recast leaves the borrower with some potentially serious complications.

Most notably, the monthly payment has increased substantially. The minimum monthly payment was $1,333 per month (first year). The fully indexed payment has climbed to $3,159.93. That's a difference of $1,826.93 every month. This amounts to a payment difference of $21,923.16 per year! This big of a payment increase can put a huge financial strain on a family. Further, this payment difference can no longer be saved and grown over time; rather, it is required to pay down the loan as an amortized payment.

An additional problem Dick and Jane face in this scenario is increasing interest rates. Their amortized monthly payment is already far higher than they were accustomed to with the minimum monthly payment. Since their interest rate is variable, the interest can go up, thereby increasing an already onerous payment. In fact, just a half a percent increase in the interest rate would increase their monthly payment by more than $140 a month.

These problems are ameliorated or eliminated entirely with the Secured Option ARM loan. When Dick and Jane reached the recast point on their Secured Option ARM loan after 5 years (or after reaching the recast point) things would look quite different than they did when they used the traditional Option ARM loan.

First, the payment difference would be gigantic. Remember, at the recast point a Secured Option ARM loan becomes an interest only loan for the next 5 years. This means that with a Secured Option ARM loan Dick and Jane's payment starting after recast would be $2,683.33 ($400,000 original loan balance + $60,000 deferred interest over 5 years = $460,000. $460,000 x 7% interest = $32,200 per year. $32,000 \ 12 months = $2,683.33 per month). This $2,683.33 interest only payment is a $476.60 monthly savings over the traditional Option ARM loan's payment of $3,159.93 monthly payment. This payment difference gives the borrower greater financial flexibility than was available using the traditional Option ARM loan. Further, it also still gives the borrowers the opportunity to save the difference between the interest only payment and the amortized payment to continue growing wealth if so desired.

Second, having the five year interest only option provides greater financial security to the borrower in a rising interest rate environment. With the traditional Option ARM loan, after recast, the borrower is left with two options. They can keep their loan which has become an amortized loan or they can refinance and get a new loan. However, with interest rates increasing, refinancing may not be an attractive option. A nice feature of the Secured Option ARM loan is that after recast the loan has until year 10 of the original loan period as an interest only period. Not only does this provide a lower payment option but it may make it easier to weather the storm of rising interest rates. Five extra years of interest only payments gives the borrower five years to wait out rising interest rates and hope they decline in order to refinance at a lower interest rate.

* * *

Upside Potential

Now that we have addressed the mechanics of the Secured Option ARM loan and examined the features that differentiate the Secured Option ARM loan from the traditional Option ARM loan, we should focus on how utilizing the Secured Option ARM loan can maximize ones potential for wealth generation.

The strategy for wealth generation using the Secured Option ARM loan is similar to the strategy outlined in the previous chapter detailing the traditional Option ARM loan. The method simply involves saving the difference between the minimum monthly payment and the 30 year amortized payment in a separate investment vehicle. While the strategy is similar, the potential wealth generation is far greater using the Secured Option ARM loan. Let's examine some numbers to demonstrate and compare.

In the previous chapter we detailed the potential wealth generation of saving the difference between the minimum monthly payment on a $400,000 loan and the 30 year amortized monthly payment. Using the same numbers from the last chapter, the minimum monthly payment was $1,333 and the 30 year amortized payment was $2,661. This left a difference of $1,328 to be saved in an investment vehicle. However, if you recall, the payment amount on the minimum monthly payment in a traditional Option ARM has the potential to go up. Assuming that the payment amount rose by the contractual maximum (which is likely) then the savings difference diminished year by year (see chart to refresh your memory of the figures).

Month 1-12: $1,333.01
Month 13-24: $1,432.98
Month 25-36: $1,540.46
Month 37-48: $1,655.99
Month 49-60: $1,780.19

Year 1 total: $15,938.44
Year 2 total: $14,738.73
Year 3 total: $13,449.05
Year 4 total: $12,062.64
Year 5 total: $10,572.25
Grand Total: $66,761.11

The savings difference utilizing the Secured Option ARM loan is not insignificant. Saving the difference between the numbers used in the Dick and Jane examples in this chapter amounts to a $1,328 monthly savings. However, unlike the traditional Option ARM loan, the payment amount on the minimum monthly payment for the Secured Option ARM loan is fixed for 5 years (or until the recast happens). The monthly savings is constant for the entire 5 year period. Quickly doing the math, the 5 year projection for saving the difference using the Secured Option ARM loan would look like this:

Month 1-12: $1,333.33	Year 1 total: $15,934.52
Month 13-24: $1,333.33	Year 2 total: $15,935.52
Month 25-36: $1,333.33	Year 3 total: $15,935.52
Month 37-48: $1,333.33	Year 4 total: $15,935.52
Month 49-60: $1,333.33	Year 5 total: $15,935.52
	Grand Total: $79,672.60

As anyone can see in examining the two charts, the traditional Option ARM loan starts out with a significant monthly and yearly savings. However, over the 5 year period it is beaten by the Secured Option ARM loan. Further, the superior performance is achieved without the borrower about keeping an eye on interest rates since the interest rate is fixed for the first 5 years. Additionally, there is no concern about early recast which could really diminish the projected returns of the traditional Option ARM loan since the recast point on the Secured Option ARM can be determined with pin-point accuracy before the loan is used. The Secured Option ARM loan wins both by maximizing upside potential and minimizing downside risk. (Figure 5.1 & 5.2)

Taking the saved money and letting it compound with interest paints an even rosier picture. Let us extrapolate the potential returns using a 4% interest rate, a 6% interest rate, and an 8% interest rate.

For the conservative investor, a nice steady return of 4% might satisfy. At the end of the first year of saving the difference at 4% interest one would have amassed $16,284.02. Jumping forward to the 5 year savings and compounding point, at a mere 4% interest, one would have amassed $88,330.82. That's more than an $8,000 difference between the total for simply saving the difference and saving the difference and compounding 4% interest. At this point, if you chose to follow the same strategy outlined with the traditional Option ARM loan and cease saving the difference and pay off your loan (although, with the Secured Option ARM loan the interest only payment option is still available after the 5 year recast which affords the borrowers further opportunity to save the difference and grow their wealth…) the potential wealth generated would extrapolate out as follows. At the end of year 10, at 4% interest, the total wealth grown would be $107,851.02. At the end of year 15, at 4% interest, the total wealth grown would be $131,685.73. At the end of year 20, at 4% interest, the total wealth grown would be $160,787.83. At the end of year 25, at 4% interest, the total wealth grown would be $196,321.39. Finally, at the end of year 30, when the loan term would be over (although there is nothing to say that you couldn't continue to allow your wealth to compound…), at 4% interest, the total wealth grown would be $239,707.75. An impressive total, especially considering that nothing was added to the principal for the last 25 years of compounding.

Traditional Option ARM Loan Example

Stan & Martha				Term (months)		360
Home Value	$500,000			Min Pay Rate		1.25%
Untapped Equity	$100,000	20%				
				Fully Indexed Rate:		7.000%
Option ARM Amt	$400,000	80%		Margin:		2.850%
				Index:		4.150%
				Recast Percent		125%

YEAR	Low Minimum Payment	Interest Only Payment	Traditional 30 Year Payment	15 Year Payment	Monthly Cash Flow	Annual Cash Flow	Monthly Deferred Interest
1	$1,333.01	$2,333.33	$2,661.21	$3,595.31	$1,328.20	$15,938.44	$1,000.33
2	$1,432.98	$2,333.33	$2,661.21	$3,595.31	$1,228.23	$14,738.73	$900.35
3	$1,540.46	$2,333.33	$2,661.21	$3,595.31	$1,120.75	$13,449.05	$792.88
4	$1,655.99	$2,333.33	$2,661.21	$3,595.31	$1,005.22	$12,062.64	$677.34
5	$1,780.19	$2,333.33	$2,661.21	$3,595.31	$881.02	$10,572.25	$553.14

Annual Deferred Interest	New Principal Balance on Loan	New House Value at 3% growth	New House Value at 5% growth
$12,003.92	$412,003.92	$515,000.00	$525,000.00
$10,804.21	$422,808.13	$530,450.00	$551,250.00
$9,514.53	$432,322.66	$546,363.50	$578,812.50
$8,128.12	$440,450.78	$562,754.41	$607,753.13
$6,637.73	$447,088.51	$579,637.04	$638,140.78

(*Figure 5.2* ~ This is a hypothetical example to illustrate the cash flow difference between the fully indexed rate and the minimum payment. There is no guarantee that the Index used will remain the same month after month. Therefore the deferred interest may be higher or lower than the illustration.)

The numbers look even more impressive at higher interest rates. At 6% interest, the first year total wealth grown would be $16,462.01. Jumping to the end of the 5 year point, at 6% interest, the total wealth grown would be $93,109.22. At the end of year 10, at 6% interest, the total wealth grown would be $125,590.39. At the end of year 15, at 6% interest, the total wealth grown would be $169,402.62. At the end of year 20, at 6% interest, the total wealth grown

Secured Option ARM Loan Example

Stan & Martha				Term (months)		360	
Home Value	$500,000						
Untapped Equity	$100,000	20%		Fully Indexed Rate:		7.000%	
				Margin:		2.850%	
Option ARM Amt:	$400,000	80%		Index:		4.150%	
				Min. Pmt Deduction		3%	
				Recast Percent		115%	

YEAR	Low Minimum Payment	Interest Only Payment	Traditional 30 Year Payment	15 Year Payment	Monthly Cash Flow	Annual Cash Flow	Monthly Deferred Interest
1	$1,333.33	$2,333.33	$2,661.21	$3,595.31	$1,327.88	$15,934.52	$1,000.00
2	$1,333.33	$2,333.33	$2,661.21	$3,595.31	$1,327.88	$15,934.52	$1,000.00
3	$1,333.33	$2,333.33	$2,661.21	$3,595.31	$1,327.88	$15,934.52	$1,000.00
4	$1,333.33	$2,333.33	$2,661.21	$3,595.31	$1,327.88	$15,934.52	$1,000.00
5	$1,333.33	$2,333.33	$2,661.21	$3,595.31	$1,327.88	$15,934.52	$1,000.00

Annual Deferred Interest	New Principal Balance on Loan	New House Value at 3% growth	New House Value at 5% growth
$12,000.00	$412,000.00	$515,000.00	$525,000.00
$12,000.00	$424,000.00	$530,450.00	$551,250.00
$12,000.00	$436,000.00	$546,363.50	$578,812.50
$12,000.00	$448,000.00	$562,754.41	$607,753.13
$12,000.00	$460,000.00	$579,637.04	$638,140.78

Figure 5.1 ~ This is a hypothetical example to illustrate the cash flow difference between the fully indexed rate and the minimum payment.)

would be $228,498.75. At the end of year 25, at 6% interest, the total wealth grown would be $308,210.57. Finally, at the end of year 30, at 6% interest, the total wealth grown would be $415,729.88. At only 2% higher interest than our 4% example, the total wealth grown is almost double that grown at 4%.

Completing our examples, we'll look at the potential outcome if an 8% interest rate was earned. At 8% interest, the first year total wealth grown would be $16,642.18.

Jumping to the 5 year point, at 8% interest, the total wealth grown would be $98,218.66. At the end of year 10, at 8% interest, the total wealth grown would be $146,330.64. At the end of year 15, at 8% interest, the total wealth grown would be $218,010.08. At the end of year 20, at 8% interest, the total wealth grown would be $324,501.38. At the end of year 25, at 8% interest, the total wealth grown would be $483,903.95. Finally, at the end of year 30, at 8% interest the total wealth grown would be $720,942.22. Nearly ¾ of a million dollars grown from a 5 year savings of only $79,673. (Figure 5.3)

* * *

The similarities between the Secured Option ARM loan and the traditional Option ARM loan are numerous. One of the similarities that we want to caution investors about, again, is how it can go wrong. Just as the strategy for growing wealth between the two types of Option ARM loans is similar, the ways people court disaster with the two loans is similar. To quickly refresh from last chapter, if one is unable to make the 30 year amortized payment at the outset, they should not take the loan. Further, if one fails to save the difference between the minimum monthly payment and the 30 year amortized payment, then that borrower is simply living beyond their means and not growing any future potential wealth. Despite these avoidable pitfalls, however, the upside potential offered through the use of the Secured Option ARM loan is incredible when a borrower is disciplined enough to invest the difference and therefore realize the gain.

	Assumed Interest Rate:	4%, 6%, 8%		
	Total Cash Flow Savings:	$79,672.80		

Year	Monthly Cash Flow Savings on New Loan	Hypothetical Growth at 4.0%	Hypothetical Growth at 6.0%	Hypothetical Growth at 8.0%
1	$1,327.88	$16,284.06	$16,462.05	$16,642.22
2	$1,327.88	$33,231.57	$33,939.44	$34,665.74
3	$1,327.88	$50,869.53	$52,494.80	$54,185.20
4	$1,327.88	$69,226.10	$72,194.61	$75,324.76
5	$1,327.88	$88,330.54	$93,109.46	$98,218.90
6		$91,929.27	$98,852.25	$106,371.02
7		$95,674.61	$104,949.24	$115,199.77
8		$99,572.54	$111,422.28	$124,761.29
9		$103,629.28	$118,294.56	$135,116.42
10		$107,851.29	$125,590.71	$146,331.01
11		$112,245.32	$133,336.87	$158,476.41
12		$116,818.37	$141,560.79	$171,629.88
13		$121,577.73	$150,291.95	$185,875.07
14		$126,530.99	$159,561.63	$201,302.61
15		$131,686.06	$169,403.05	$218,010.63
16		$137,051.16	$179,851.46	$236,105.41
17		$142,634.83	$190,944.30	$255,702.04
18		$148,445.99	$202,721.33	$276,925.18
19		$154,493.91	$215,224.73	$299,909.84
20		$160,788.23	$228,499.32	$324,802.20
21		$167,338.99	$242,592.66	$351,760.63
22		$174,156.64	$257,555.25	$380,956.58
23		$181,252.05	$273,440.69	$412,575.79
24		$188,636.54	$290,305.92	$446,819.38
25		$196,321.89	$308,211.35	$483,905.17
26		$204,320.34	$327,221.15	$524,069.06
27		$212,644.67	$347,403.43	$567,566.53
28		$221,308.14	$368,830.52	$614,674.28
29		$230,324.57	$391,579.18	$665,691.94
30		$239,708.35	$415,730.92	$720,944.04

(*Figure 5.3* ~ Growth of the savings at 4, 6, & 8% generated during the first 5 years by the difference between the minimum payment and the 30 year payment.)

Chapter 6
Buying a New Home

Chapter 6
Buying a New Home

The case for tremendous potential wealth generation has been made abundantly clear at this point. Through the use of an interest only, traditional Option ARM, or Secured Option ARM loan home owners can amass huge fortunes by saving the difference and allowing interest to compound. However, so far we have only demonstrated this strategy for people looking to refinance an existing home. What about a person who was looking to purchase a new home? Are the same strategies still in play? What about down payments? What exactly ought one do? Let's examine the different scenarios.

* * *

The Story of Phillip Anderson

A few years ago a client who we will call Phillip Anderson walked through my door. His story was similar to many clients I'd seen previously and many I've seen since. Phillip was looking to purchase a house, but his loan officer told him to talk to me first. At our first meeting I asked him to tell me about his financial situation and what he and his family were looking to do.

Phillip and his family were looking to buy a house. Having lived in a small apartment for several years, they had saved up $25,000 to use as a down payment and were ready to buy their piece of the American dream. Living in California where real estate prices have gone berserk, Phillip had found a nice three bedroom, two bath condo in a nice neighborhood for $500,000. He had done a little bit of research and shopping for mortgages, so I asked him what he was thinking.

Phillip was convinced that his best option (actually, he was convinced it was his only option...) was to acquire what is commonly referred to as an 80/15/5 loan. The simple idea is that the borrower will make a 5% down payment, take out a 1st mortgage for 80% of the value of the house, and a 2nd mortgage for the remaining 15%. In Phillip's case, to purchase his $500,000 home, he was prepared to put $25,000 as his 5% down, take out a $400,000 1st, and a $75,000 2nd.

Phillip seemed pleased that he had found a way to move out of his apartment and into his own home, but I could tell he was frustrated with what seemed to him to be his only option. Phillip had delayed looking into home ownership because he had originally believed that a 20% down payment was required. Once he had discovered that there were other options that would require a smaller down payment, he began to look for prospective homes. However, even though he had found an alternative to coming up with a 20% down payment, as we talked he admitted that putting up the $25,000 was a bit frightening as he realized how long it had taken him to save it. At this point it was time to show Phillip that he definitely had some options before he purchased his new home.

Most people in Phillip's situation think just like Phillip. They have been raised to believe that home purchases require a 20% down payment. While this is true for most mortgages in order to avoid paying mortgage insurance, it is not particularly difficult to find finance options for home loans with less than 20% down and that allow the borrower to avoid costly mortgage insurance.

Further, the conventional wisdom, as we've discussed previously, tells people to pay off their homes quickly. This further leads people to believe that a big down payment (or any down payment for that matter!) is important.

I began to help Phillip first by examining the payment amounts he would be looking at if he purchased the home he was interested in using the 80/15/5 mortgage he was considering. On Phillip's $500,000 loan he would be looking at a $400,000 1st mortgage (80% of the $500,000 purchase price), a $75,000 2nd mortgage (15% of the $500,000 purchase price), and a $25,000 down payment (5% of the purchase price). I reminded Phillip that rates for 1st mortgages are generally lower than rates for 2nd mortgages and we looked at the current rates at the time (keep in mind, this was a few years back). A $400,000 1st mortgage he could get at 7% and the $75,000 2nd would be at 10%. So, his monthly payment would come to $2,661.21 on his 1st mortgage and $658.18 on his 2nd. Combined Phillip was looking at a monthly payment of $3,319.39.

At this point I brought up the $25,000 down payment. I knew this was the sore spot with Phillip so I thought it would be the best thing to address first. I asked him if he would be interested in looking at the payment numbers for his mortgage with 100% financing. I told him that 100% financing was possible given his financial situation so we ran the numbers. Using the same $500,000 home loan, but eliminating the $25,000 down payment, the 1st mortgage payment stayed the exact same at $2,661.21. The 2nd mortgage, however, was for $100,000 at 11% instead of $75,000 at 10%. This resulted in a new payment of $952.32 per month. This amounted to a $294.14 monthly increase by taking the zero down payment option (in his situation he would also not have to pay mortgage insurance).

Seeing the numbers, Phillip told me that he could afford the extra $294.14 a month, but he liked the lower monthly payment that the $25,000 down payment brought. It was my turn to be surprised. It was clear that Phillip saw the connection between the down payment and a lower monthly payment. However, Phillip needed a little lesson on what he was giving up to get that small monthly payment reduction. Specifically, Phillip needed to see that if he made that $25,000 down payment he would be making three potentially significant mistakes: 1) He would be losing a $25,000 asset, 2) He would be putting his $25,000 into a non-liquid environment, and 3) It would take him years to make back the $25,000 by saving the difference between the monthly payment on the 80/15/5 loan and the 100% financed loan.

* * *

Down Payment as a Lost Asset

If Phillip put his $25,000 as a down payment, that money would be lost as a wealth building asset. It is true that he would have $25,000 in equity at the time of purchasing his house. However, there is no guarantee that the equity would remain. Home values tend to rise in the United States, but they do go down. It would be entirely possible for Phillip to lose that $25,000 in equity with just a mild drop in home values.

However, even if home values increased, as we've talked about previously, equity earns no interest. The $25,000 Phillip would have spent on a down payment could have been put to use earning interest and allowing it to compound and grow. Investing that $25,000 at 8% interest for the life of the 30 year loan would yield a return of

$251,566.42 (compounded annually). That is a lot of potential wealth generation to miss out on in exchange for simply accruing a non-performing asset like equity.

* * *

Down Payment Loses Liquidity

While missing out on the potential wealth generation is a huge factor, another potentially negative factor that Phillip might have had to face as a result of making the down payment would be the loss of liquidity regarding that $25,000 down payment.

If Phillip used the $25,000 as a down payment, that money would become equity in the house he bought. However, that money would be essentially trapped becoming very difficult to get at. A frightening scenario arises if Phillip is confronted with losing his job. Without an income, it would become difficult for Phillip to qualify for a loan. So, even though he has equity sitting in his house, he could potentially be unable to get at it.

In this scenario the liquidity of Phillip's $25,000 is reduced as a result of it being locked away as equity. Not only is he not earning interest, but his access to his money is difficult, if not outright impossible.

* * *

Down Payment Reduces the Monthly Payment by an Amount that Would Take Years to Recoup

Perhaps the most difficult negative factor for Phillip (and most people) to see is that while the $25,000 down payment does reduce the monthly payment, the amount it reduces the payment by would take an enormous amount of time to grow back.

In Phillip's example, the monthly payment (for both the 1st and 2nd mortgages added together) with the $25,000 down payment was $3,319.39. The monthly payment without the $25,000 down payment was $3,613.14. The monthly difference amounts to $294.14. $25,000 of Phillip's hard earned money had to be used to get that monthly payment reduction of $294.14. To make that $25,000 back just saving the $294.14 each month would take Phillip just days under 85 months! That's basically 7 years and change to make the $25,000 back. That's a pretty slow return on investment on the $25,000 down payment.

* * *

Phillip's Decision

Having explained the difference between making a down payment and financing the whole loan, Phillip seemed pretty convinced that having easy access to his safe, liquid asset of $25,000 would be advantageous. Phillip opted for the traditional Option ARM loan for the 1st loan (Secured Option ARM loans were not available when he purchased his house) and an interest only payment for the 2nd. Choosing the traditional Option ARM loan gave Phillip the opportunity to exercise the minimum monthly payment option in order to save the difference between the traditional 30 year payment and the minimum monthly payment. On top of saving the difference, Phillip used his $25,000 to further enhance his wealth generating potential.

* * *

Evaluating Phillip's Decision and Assessing the Alternatives

Phillip's decision has paid off in spades for him and his family. Utilizing the minimum monthly payment of the traditional Option ARM loan has allowed Phillip and his family to save a considerable sum over the past several years. Add to the pot the $25,000 he didn't use as a down payment and Phillip is well on his way to having a nice nest egg for his children's college education, future home improvement, or retirement. However, while Phillip opted for the Option ARM loan several options are available to others, each with upside potential. Bearing in mind that not all families will qualify for all loan options the lesion to be learned from Phillip's scenario is that the least amount of your own money used as a down payment generates the best financial footing. Let us examine the various possible routes one could take and the potential growth each could yield.

On the following pages, the same interest rates are used for the Traditional Option ARM, Secured Option ARM, and 10 Year Interest Only Loans. The likelihood of these very different loan scenarios having the same interest rate is very remote. We have chosen to use the same interest rate for all three loans purely for the sake of illustrating how each loan can be used to accumulate wealth outside of the home. Consult your financial professional to see which scenario, if any, would be right for you.

Traditional Option ARM Loan Scenario

Phillip Anderson					Term (months)		360
Home Value	$500,000				Min Pay Rate		1.25%
2nd Loan	$100,000	20%			Fully Indexed Rate:		7.00%
					Margin:		2.85%
Option ARM Amt	$400,000	80%			Index:		4.15%
					Recast Percent		125%

YEAR	Low Minimum Payment	Interest Only Payment	Traditional 30 Year Payment	15 Year Payment	Monthly Cash Flow	Annual Cash Flow	Monthly Deferred Interest
1	$1,333.01	$2,333.33	$2,661.21	$3,595.31	$1,328.20	$15,938.44	$1,000.3
2	$1,432.98	$2,333.33	$2,661.21	$3,595.31	$1,228.23	$14,738.73	$900.35
3	$1,540.46	$2,333.33	$2,661.21	$3,595.31	$1,120.75	$13,449.05	$792.88
4	$1,655.99	$2,333.33	$2,661.21	$3,595.31	$1,005.22	$12,062.64	$677.34
5	$1,780.19	$2,333.33	$2,661.21	$3,595.31	$881.02	$10,572.25	$553.14

Phillip Anderson				Term (months)		360
Home Value	$500,000			Interest Only Pmt		11.00%
Option ARM Amt	$400,000	80%		Fully Indexed Rate:		11.00%
				Margin:		2.50%
2nd Loan	$100,000	20%		Index: Prime @		8.50%

YEAR	Interest Only Payment	Traditional 30 Year Payment	Monthly Cash Flow	Annual Cash Flow	Monthly Deferred Interest
1	$916.67	$952.32	$35.66	$427.88	0
2	$916.67	$952.32	$35.66	$427.88	0
3	$916.67	$952.32	$35.66	$427.88	0
4	$916.67	$952.32	$35.66	$427.88	0
5	$916.67	$952.32	$35.66	$427.88	0

Annual Deferred Interest	New Principal Balance on Loan	New House Value at 3% growth	New House Value at 5% growth	80/15 Proposed Payment	Total Monthly Starting Payment	Recast Payment
$12,003.92	$512,003.92	$515,000.00	$525,000.00	$3,319.39	$2,249.67	$4,076.6
$10,804.21	$522,808.13	$530,450.00	$551,250.00			
$9,514.53	$532,322.66	$546,363.50	$578,812.50			
$8,128.12	$540,450.78	$562,754.41	$607,753.13			
$6,637.73	$547,088.51	$579,637.04	$638,140.78			

(*Figure 6.1* ~ Since the Index is a variable rate that can change monthly, the interest rate may be higher or lower on a monthly basis. This means that the amount of deferred interest could be more or less than the illustration and the recast point may happen before the end of the 5th year. In addition, the recast payment illustrated may be more or less depending on the amount of deferred interest added to the loan and the current index rate at the time of recast. The recast payment illustrates an interest only payment on the second which is typical until the 10th year.)

Buying a New Home - 119

Assumed Interest Rate					6%
Starting Lump Sum					$25,000
Total Cash Flow Savings Between Minimum Payment and Amortized Payment					$66,761.04
Difference Between 2nd I.O. Payment and Amortized Payment (1st 5 years)					$2,139.60
				Total Investment over 5 Years:	$93,900.64
Year	Lump Sum Contribution	Monthly Cash Flow Savings on 1st Loan	Monthly Cash Flow Savings on 2nd Loan	Monthly Cash Flow Savings 1st & 2nd	Hypothetical Growth at 6%
1	$25,000.00	$1,328.20	$35.66	$1,363.86	$43,450.05
2		$1,228.23	$35.66	$1,263.89	$61,798.70
3		$1,120.75	$35.66	$1,156.41	$79,946.60
4		$1,005.22	$35.66	$1,040.88	$97,781.57
5		$881.02	$35.66	$916.68	$115,176.82
6					$122,280.68
7					$129,822.68
8					$137,829.86
9					$146,330.91
10					$155,356.28
11					$164,938.31
12					$175,111.35
13					$185,911.83
14					$197,378.47
15					$209,552.34
16					$222,477.07
17					$236,198.97
18					$250,767.20
19					$266,233.97
20					$282,654.70
21					$300,088.23
22					$318,597.01
23					$338,247.38
24					$359,109.73
25					$381,258.84
26					$404,774.05
27					$429,739.63
28					$456,245.03
29					$484,385.22
30					$514,261.04

(Figure 6.2 ~ This illustration assumes a constant rate of return of 6% with no transaction costs or taxes assessed. Investments don't typically produce the same results year after year. Actual results may be better or worse than the illustration.)

Secured Option ARM Loan Scenario

Phillip Anderson					Term (months)		360
Home Value	$500,000				Min Pay Rate		4.00%
2nd Loan	$100,000	20%			Fully Indexed Rate:		7.00%
					Margin:		2.85%
Option ARM Amt	$400,000	80%			Index:		4.15%
					Recast Percent		115%

YEAR	Low Minimum Payment	Interest Only Payment	Traditional 30 Year Payment	15 Year Payment	Monthly Cash Flow	Annual Cash Flow	Monthly Deferred Interest
1	$1,333.33	$2,333.33	$2,661.21	$3,595.31	$1,327.88	$15,934.52	$1,000.0
2	$1,333.33	$2,333.33	$2,661.21	$3,595.31	$1,327.88	$15,934.52	$1,000.0
3	$1,333.33	$2,333.33	$2,661.21	$3,595.31	$1,327.88	$15,934.52	$1,000.0
4	$1,333.33	$2,333.33	$2,661.21	$3,595.31	$1,327.88	$15,934.52	$1,000.0
5	$1,333.33	$2,333.33	$2,661.21	$3,595.31	$1,327.88	$15,934.52	$1,000.0

Phillip Anderson				Term (months)		360
Home Value	$500,000			Interest Only Pmt		11.00%
Option ARM Amt	$400,000	80%		Fully Indexed Rate:		11.00%
				Margin:		2.50%
2nd Loan	$100,000	20%		Index: Prime @		8.50%

YEAR		Interest Only Payment	Traditional 30 Year Payment		Monthly Cash Flow	Annual Cash Flow	Monthly Deferred Interest
1		$916.67	$952.32		$35.66	$427.88	0
2		$916.67	$952.32		$35.66	$427.88	0
3		$916.67	$952.32		$35.66	$427.88	0
4		$916.67	$952.32		$35.66	$427.88	0
5		$916.67	$952.32		$35.66	$427.88	0

Annual Deferred Interest	New Principal Balance on Loan	New House Value at 3% growth	New House Value at 5% growth	80/15 Proposed Payment	Total Monthly Starting Payment	Recast Payment
$12,000.00	$412,000.00	$515,000.00	$525,000.00	$3,319.39	$2,250.00	$3,600.0
$12,000.00	$424,000.00	$530,450.00	$551,250.00			
$12,000.00	$436,000.00	$546,363.50	$578,812.50			
$12,000.00	$448,000.00	$562,754.41	$607,753.13			
$12,000.00	$460,000.00	$579,637.04	$638,140.78			

(*Figure 6.3* ~ The recast point may happen before the end of the 5th year if too much interest is deferred. In addition, the recast payment illustrated may be more or less depending on the current interest rates after the fixed period (typically 5 years) has expired. The recast payment will be an interest only payment on the 1st and 2nd until the end of the 10th year from the start of the loan. Interest rates will typically adjust biannually or annually after the 5th year.)

Assumed Interest Rate					6%
Starting Lump Sum					$25,000
Total Cash Flow Savings Between Minimum Payment and Amortized Payment					$79,672.80
Difference Between 2nd I.O. Payment and Amortized Payment (1st 5 years)					$2,139.60
				Total Investment over 5 years:	$106,812.40
Year	Lump Sum Contribution	Monthly Cash Flow Savings on 1st Loan	Monthly Cash Flow Savings on 2nd Loan	Monthly Cash Flow Savings 1st & 2nd	Hypothetical Growth at 6%
1	$25,000.00	$1,327.88	$35.66	$1,363.54	$43,446.08
2		$1,327.88	$35.66	$1,363.54	$63,029.87
3		$1,327.88	$35.66	$1,363.54	$83,821.55
4		$1,327.88	$35.66	$1,363.54	$105,895.61
5		$1,327.88	$35.66	$1,363.54	$129,331.15
6					$137,308.01
7					$145,776.87
8					$154,768.07
9					$164,313.83
10					$174,448.34
11					$185,207.94
12					$196,631.16
13					$208,758.94
14					$221,634.73
15					$235,304.68
16					$249,817.75
17					$265,225.97
18					$281,584.52
19					$298,952.04
20					$317,390.75
21					$336,966.72
22					$357,750.08
23					$379,815.33
24					$403,241.51
25					$428,112.56
26					$454,517.61
27					$482,551.26
28					$512,313.96
29					$543,912.37
30					$577,459.69

(Figure 6.4 ~ This illustration assumes a constant rate of return of 6% with no transaction costs or taxes assessed. Investments don't typically produce the same results year after year. Actual results may be better or worse than the illustration.)

122 - The New Mortgage Investment Advisor

10 Year Interest Only Loan

Phillip Anderson				Term (months)		360
Home Value	$500,000			Min Pay Rate		4.00%
2nd Loan	$100,000	20%		Fully Indexed Rate:		7.00%
				Margin:		2.85%
Option ARM Amt	$400,000	80%		Index:		4.15%
				Recast Percent		115%

YEAR	Interest Only Payment	Traditional 30 Year Payment	Monthly Cash Flow	Annual Cash Flow	Monthly Deferred Interest
1	$2,333.33	$2,661.21	$327.88	$3,934.52	$0.00
2	$2,333.33	$2,661.21	$327.88	$3,934.52	$0.00
3	$2,333.33	$2,661.21	$327.88	$3,934.52	$0.00
4	$2,333.33	$2,661.21	$327.88	$3,934.52	$0.00
5	$2,333.33	$2,661.21	$327.88	$3,934.52	$0.00
6	$2,333.33	$2,661.21	$327.88	$3,934.52	$0.00
7	$2,333.33	$2,661.21	$327.88	$3,934.52	$0.00
8	$2,333.33	$2,661.21	$327.88	$3,934.52	$0.00
9	$2,333.33	$2,661.21	$327.88	$3,934.52	$0.00
10	$2,333.33	$2,661.21	$327.88	$3,934.52	$0.00

Phillip Anderson				Term (months)		360
Home Value	$500,000			Interest Only Pmt		11.00%
Option ARM Amt	$400,000	80%		Fully Indexed Rate:		11.00%
				Margin:		2.50%
2nd Loan	$100,000	20%		Index: Prime @		8.50%

YEAR	Interest Only Payment	Traditional 30 Year Payment	Monthly Cash Flow	Annual Cash Flow	Monthly Deferred Interest
1	$916.67	$952.32	$35.66	$427.88	$0.00
2	$916.67	$952.32	$35.66	$427.88	$0.00
3	$916.67	$952.32	$35.66	$427.88	$0.00
4	$916.67	$952.32	$35.66	$427.88	$0.00
5	$916.67	$952.32	$35.66	$427.88	$0.00
6	$916.67	$952.32	$35.66	$427.88	$0.00
7	$916.67	$952.32	$35.66	$427.88	$0.00
8	$916.67	$952.32	$35.66	$427.88	$0.00
9	$916.67	$952.32	$35.66	$427.88	$0.00
10	$916.67	$952.32	$35.66	$427.88	$0.00

YEAR	New Principal Balance on Loan	New House Value at 3% growth	New House Value at 5% growth	80/15 Proposed Payment	Total Monthly Starting Payment	Recast Payment
1	$500,000.00	$515,000.00	$525,000.00	$3,319.39	$3,250.00	$4,133.38
5	$500,000.00	$579,637.04	$638,140.78			
10	$500,000.00	$671,958.19	$814,447.31			

(*Figure 6.5* ~ This illustrates a 10 Year Interest Only Loan that will be paid off in 30 years. The first 10 years have a fixed interest rate for both the 1st and the 2nd. After the first 10 years, the interest rate will adjust biannually or annually to match the current rate for the indexes the loans are tied too. The recast payment may be higher or lower depending on the current rates.)

Buying a New Home - 123

Assumed Interest Rate					6%
Starting Lump Sum					$25,000
Total Cash Flow Savings Between Interest Only Payment and Amortized Payment					$39,345.60
Difference Between 2nd I.O. Payment and Amortized Payment (1st 10 years)					$51,345.60
			Total Investment over 5 Years		
Year	Lump Sum Contribution	Monthly Cash Flow Savings on 1st Loan	Monthly Cash Flow Savings on 2nd Loan	Monthly Cash Flow Savings 1st & 2nd	Hypothetical Growth at 6%
1	$25,000.00	$327.88	$35.66	$363.54	$31,048.84
2		$327.88	$35.66	$363.54	$37,470.76
3		$327.88	$35.66	$363.54	$44,288.76
4		$327.88	$35.66	$363.54	$51,527.29
5		$327.88	$35.66	$363.54	$59,212.27
6		$327.88	$35.66	$363.54	$67,371.25
7		$327.88	$35.66	$363.54	$76,033.45
8		$327.88	$35.66	$363.54	$85,229.92
9		$327.88	$35.66	$363.54	$94,993.61
10		$327.88	$35.66	$363.54	$105,359.50
11					$111,857.84
12					$118,756.99
13					$126,081.66
14					$133,858.10
15					$142,114.18
16					$150,879.47
17					$160,185.38
18					$170,065.27
19					$180,554.52
20					$191,690.73
21					$203,513.79
22					$216,066.08
23					$229,392.56
24					$243,540.99
25					$258,562.07
26					$274,509.61
27					$291,440.76
28					$309,416.19
29					$328,500.31
30					$348,761.49

(*Figure 6.6* ~ This illustration assumes a constant rate of return of 6% with no transaction costs or taxes assessed. Investments don't typically produce the same results year after year. Actual results may be better or worse than the illustration.)

Chapter 7
Where to Put the Extra Money

Chapter 7
Where to Put the Extra Money

Over the course of our discussion we've outlined several strategies for utilizing varying home loans, saving the difference between amortized payments and interest only or low monthly payments, and reaping potentially huge rewards. Convincing people that the conventional wisdom of paying down their home loan might not be the best financial strategy takes time and lots of examples. However, if you've made it this far into the book, then odds are you are convinced that there is potential in the strategies we've outlined. The one part of the strategy that we still have not properly addressed is where to invest the money accumulated by saving the difference between payments.

Before we get into the specific places to put the savings, we should remind the reader that the strategies discussed are long-term strategies that are of primary use in saving towards retirement. Before implementation of any of the strategies outlined in this book, consult your financial, legal, and/or tax professional first. If your goal is to simply make a few thousand bucks quickly to purchase a new car or some other luxury, there might be better strategies for you to consider. However, since all of us realize we have a finite amount of time to spend in our careers and we all want to enjoy our golden years to their fullest, the time to prepare for retirement is now.

***
Four Phases of Retirement

As the Baby Boom generation prepares to enter their retirement years, they would be wise to recall a popular song of their youth. Made famous in the music industry (although our Biblically astute readers will recognize that the inspiration for the lyrics came from the Old Testament Book of Ecclesiastes) by a band called The Byrds in 1965, the song was simply titled "Turn! Turn! Turn!" The lyrics to the song are simple, yet profound. They simply point out that there is a season for every activity of man. There is a time to be born and a time to die. There is a time to laugh and a time to mourn. There is a time to sow and a time to reap. For our purposes of investing, this last is the key lyric.

Retirement is not something that simply happens. It is the time when we reap from what we have sown. People who do not sow or sow poorly will have little or nothing to reap. People who do not plan or plan poorly for retirement will have little or nothing upon which to retire. Fortunately, with proper planning, retirement can be a season to look forward to, not to dread.

When preparing for retirement, there are four periods to consider. Each of these periods is chronological and cannot be skipped. Ignoring any of these periods will spell some sort of trouble for the retiree. The four phases, in order, are:

1) Contribution
2) Accumulation
3) Withdrawal
4) Transfer

***
Contribution

The contribution period is where the retirement plan begins. This period is usually the longest period in that it, ideally, should last the entire length of one's working years. It is during this period that investors make their contributions to their retirement accounts. These accounts can be funded through either single payments (often called "lump sums") or periodic (weekly, monthly, annually) deposits. The contribution period (sometimes known as the investment period) is where the investor is sowing in preparation for a fruitful retirement harvest.

***
Accumulation

The money in the specific investment accounts grow through a rate of return. While the single payments or periodic deposits we make are the key to providing the capital to invest, it is the accumulation period that allows the deposits to grow through compound interest. The longer the period that an investment has to grow and the higher the rate of return earned, the greater the profit when one finally retires. This being the case, the prudent investor begins planning for retirement early in their working years to allow time to work for him.

***
Withdrawal

The third stage in retirement planning is the withdrawal period. This is the focus for most people when it comes to retirement. It is this period in which the investor begins to pull out money from his investments in which to live on. If properly planned for, the investor can withdraw a steady income for the rest of their life. If poorly planned (usually linked to skimping on the contribution period, improper vehicles for the accumulation period, or poor tax planning for the withdrawal period) the investor can anticipate a delayed or meager retirement.

* * *

Transfer

Most people think of the withdrawal period as the final stage of the retirement planning process. In a sense, this is accurate as it relates specifically to the retiree. However, most of us have children, grandchildren, churches, charitable causes, or any number of other things that are near and dear to us. While we will all eventually depart this Earth, most of us want to leave our hard earned savings to the people and things that matter most to us. This being the case, the fourth period of the retirement process is known as the transfer period. It is during this period that the retiree's assets are transferred to someone else. If properly planned for, the people or organizations that are important to the retiree can enjoy a wonderful windfall. If not properly planned for, the inheritors may suffer a loss of significant proportions, with most of this loss coming as a result of taxes and other government confiscation.

Now that the four periods of retirement have been explained we should examine the goals for investors at each period of retirement in order to maximize returns.

***
Quick Funding During Contribution Period

The contribution period is where investors set aside money towards retirement. As mentioned, the two methods for doing this are either single payments (lump sums) or periodic deposits. The goal is to put as much money into the retirement account as quickly as possible, often called "quick funding". The rationale is simple- getting more money in early allows for the account to grow more quickly. An example will clarify.

Say we have two investors, Mike and Tom. Both are 35 years old and plan on retiring at 65. Realizing they have 30 years to get their retirement plans in order, Mike decides to make a one time investment of $100,000, while Tom decides to make periodic payments of $278 per month every month for 30 years. At the end of 30 years both will have put in the same amount of money towards retirement ($100,000). However, assuming they both earn the exact same rate of return (we'll assume an 8% rate of return) Mike will have amassed $1,006,265.69! Tom, on the other hand, will have made $408,145.82. While $400,000 is nothing to sneeze at, the difference is clear. By getting the money in as quickly as possible the investor has more time to allow compound interest to grow their investment. Dollar for dollar, it is far more economical to invest with a single lump sum than to spread it out over long periods of time.

***
Compound the Contribution During Accumulation Period

During the accumulation period the goal is to earn a high rate of return so that our contributions compound as quickly as possible into larger and larger amounts. The compounding of our investment dollars can be more easily understood by examining the Rule of 72 again.

Mike invested his $100,000 and received a rate of return of 8%. To calculate how long it will take Mike to double his $100,000 using the Rule of 72, 72 would be divided by 8 (8 being the rate of return). 72 divided by 8 is 9. The result, 9, is the number of years it would take for Mike to double his investment.

One factor that many people miss regarding this rule is that higher interest not only allows an investment to double faster, it allows for more periods of doubling to occur. Let us return to our example with Mike.

We just saw that it would take Mike 9 years to double his $100,000 at 8% interest into $200,000 (72 divided by 8 = 9 years). It stands to reason that if Mike could only earn 4% interest that it would take him double the time to double his $100,000. Following the formula of the Rule of 72 proves this. (72 divided by 4 = 18 years.) While most people understand this intuitively, they often forget that their accumulation period is finite. Most investors have 30 years (or less!) to allow interest to compound. Higher interest rates allow more periods to double. At 4% interest Mike can double his money every 18 years. That means that if he starts young he can double his $100,000 to $200,000 by middle age. If he works into his senior years he might be able to wait out the time it take to double his money once more. At the end of 36 years he would have $400,000.

The assumption that most people make at this point is that if Mike made $400,000 at 4% interest then he would make $800,000 at 8% interest. People often think that if they double the rate of return they simply double the end result. This is false! Keep in mind, doubling the interest allows for quicker accumulation and more periods of doubling to occur. To illustrate, using the Rule of 72, Mike invests his $100,000 again but this time at 8% interest. Instead of taking 16 years to double, it now takes 9 years. That means that if he invests for the same 36 years that he did in the first example instead of doubling his money twice, he will double it 4 times! The result is that at the end of 36 years he will have approximately $1,600,000 instead of $400,000.

* * *

Tax-Free Income During Withdrawal Period

One of the largest problems facing the financial planning industry is the misinformed and ill prepared financial planner regarding retirement income planning. Rather than seeing retirement planning as a four stage process, many planners consider the task one of simply focusing on wealth accumulation. The reasons for this are simple. Most planners are compensated by a piece of the money under the management of the planner; therefore, it behooves the planner to focus their efforts on maximizing their client's accumulation of wealth. The good news is that this focus tends to benefit both the planner and the client in regards to wealth accumulation. The client is happy because they see great returns on their investments and steadily increase their wealth. The planner is happy because they are compensated handsomely for helping to steer their client into the great returns they are receiving. The bad news, however, is that this single-minded focus on accumulation often leaves the client high and dry when it comes to the other periods of retirement planning, especially the withdrawal period.

Again, financial planners tend to focus their efforts on growing assets, not on spending assets down. Unfortunately, if wise planning is not considered regarding how to spend down assets, investors may find themselves neglecting one of the major factors that investors need to focus on during the withdrawal period.

During the withdrawal period the most important goal to strive for is the minimization of one's tax burden. It is very important to consider the amount of tax burden that will be inherited as a result of withdrawing funds. The tax factor is so often ignored or misunderstood. It is this factor that accounts for the greatest loss of anticipated revenue at the withdrawal period. Let us illustrate.

Most of us have had a financial planner or advisor at some point tell us not to worry about taxes during retirement. The argument they construct is that we will not be earning a paycheck; therefore, we will be in a lower tax bracket. However, this isn't necessarily an accurate accounting of what awaits most of us. For those preparing for retirement, they are expecting some form of retirement compensation from their employer or the government or both (social security, pension, etc.). These monies are taxable to an extent. Many people are also saving on their own, often using vehicles such as 401k programs and IRAs. The attraction is that the money invested is made with pre-income tax dollars. The downside is that the tax burden will hit when the money is withdrawn. Another tax factor is that many people who own homes will have paid off their mortgage by retirement, eliminating their number one tax deduction entirely.

We do many seminars every month throughout the United States. On occasion we will have financial planners, CPAs, enrolled agents, etc. in the audience. At one particular

Where to Put the Extra Money - 135

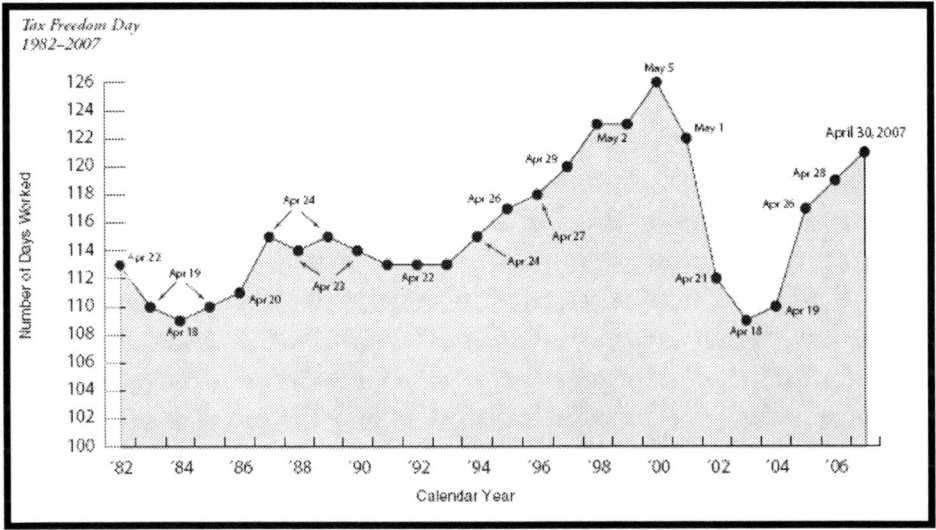

(Figure 7.1) ~ Tax Freedom Day is the day at which you have worked enough to pay for your estimated share of Federal, State and local taxes. This chart is used from the information provided at The Tax Foundation at http://www.taxfoundation.org/taxfreedomday/.)

event, we put one of the tax professionals on the spot and asked him to answer one simple question. The question was, "Do you have any clients that have retired in a lower tax bracket?" His reply was simple and to the point. "No. Not if they did their job right!" The simple point is the only people to retire in a lower tax bracket are those who don't have enough money during retirement. Many people were told that they would retire in a lower tax bracket but with all of the changes to the tax code over the last 20 years, I have not once met one tax professional who has told me that they feel their clients will retire in a lower tax bracket by choice.

A final grim factor to consider is the historical trend in this country regarding taxes. Unfortunately, history demonstrates that the government tends to raise taxes over time, not reduce them. At the outset of the United States there was no such thing as an income tax. When the income tax was originally instituted it was promised that it would only be placed on the top income earners in the U.S. and that they would only be taxed on a small portion of their earnings. Fast forward to the present and we see that the vast majority of Americans have some sort of income tax burden. Further, the burden tends to increase over time (with a few minor exceptions to the trend) as government lays claim to an ever increasing amount of our labor. Even if all the other factors mentioned were not a part of the equation, the likelihood that our tax burden will be greater years down the road is high given the historical evidence. The point being made is that the idea of having less tax burden when one retires is unlikely at best, if not purely fantasy at worst.

***

Income-Tax Free Inheritance During Transfer Period

Taxes again are the key issue during the transfer period of retirement. After sacrificing during the contribution period, waiting patiently during the accumulation period, and spending prudently during the withdrawal period, the last thing anyone wants is to surrender their investment to more taxes rather than their loved ones or the causes and organizations that are important to them. Unfortunately, taxes are always looming, waiting to prey on the unprepared. A perfect example of this lack of preparation awaits many Americans who have utilized 401ks and traditional IRAs. These investment vehicles are counted when Federal estate taxes are considered at the time of their transfer to the next generation. However, since no income tax has been paid on these dollars, the inheritor will receive what is left after the estate tax as well as pay income tax on these monies as they are withdrawn. This is referred to as the one-two punch. A properly constructed retirement plan will address how to pass on your estate with the minimum possible loss to taxes.

* * *

Choosing an Investment Vehicle

Now that the periods of retirement and the goals for each period have been outlined, it is proper to discuss which investment vehicle to use during the accumulation period of retirement. Remember, it is during the accumulation period that the contribution one makes towards retirement grows. Choosing the right vehicle for the investment can make a significant difference in the value of the investment when the withdrawal period comes. Unfortunately, many people get bogged down by the numerous investment vehicles competing for our attention. Fortunately, we believe we can provide clarity on how to choose where to place your money.

Financial professionals dicker over the exact number, but in the financial industry many would concede that there are basically 21 distinct genres of investment vehicles (Figure 7.2). Many are familiar to non-professionals like stocks, bonds, and savings accounts. Others are fairly sophisticated and used only by large corporations in specialized situations. However, while the number of different types of investment vehicles is a curious piece of trivia, the important factor is that all investments examine three crucial criteria in order to determine if they meet the needs of the investor. Ideally one would seek out an investment that fulfills all three criteria perfectly. However, we live in a less than ideal world. Realistically an investor

138 - The New Mortgage Investment Advisor

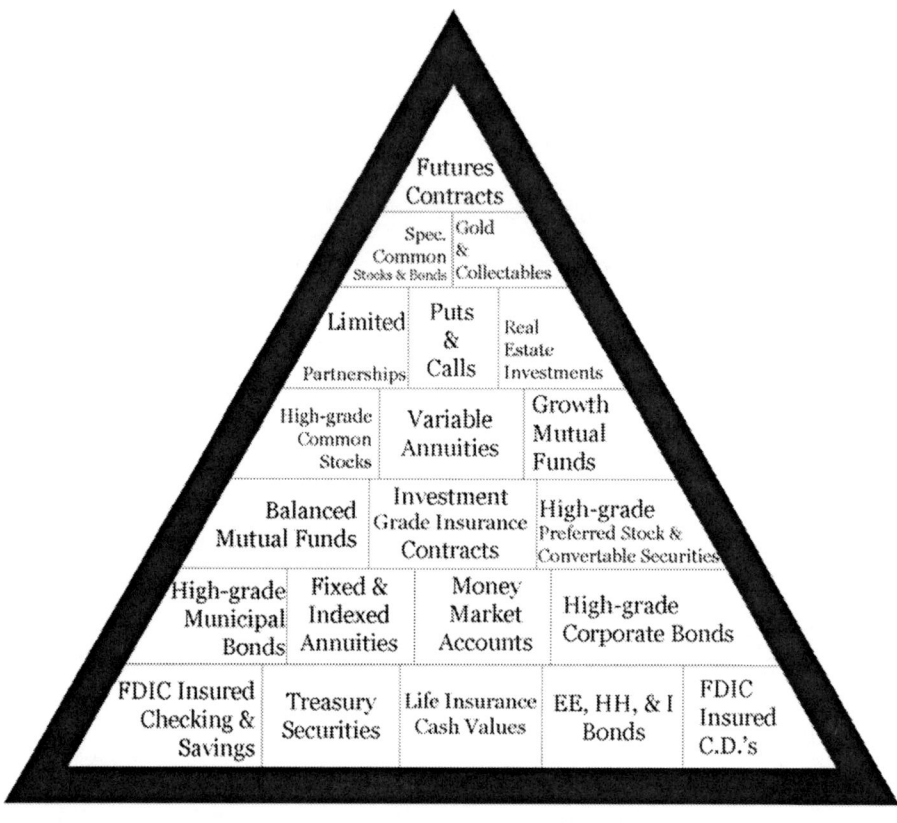

```
                    Futures
                    Contracts
              Spec.  Gold
              Common  &
              Stocks & Bonds  Collectables
        Limited  Puts
                  &      Real
        Partnerships  Calls  Estate
                              Investments
                                 Growth
        High-grade  Variable   Mutual
        Common      Annuities  Funds
        Stocks
                    Investment    High-grade
        Balanced    Grade Insurance  Preferred Stock &
        Mutual Funds  Contracts   Convertable Securities
        High-grade  Fixed &   Money
        Municipal   Indexed   Market    High-grade
        Bonds       Annuities Accounts  Corporate Bonds
        FDIC Insured  Treasury   Life Insurance  EE, HH, & I  FDIC
        Checking &    Securities Cash Values     Bonds        Insured
        Savings                                               C.D.'s
```

(*Figure 7.2* ~ The 21 most common investments are listed above. The higher the investment is in the pyramid the higher the risk associated with loss of principal as well as the higher potential for capital appreciation. The lower the investment to the pyramid's base, the safety of principal increases, but the risk of loss of purchasing power increases.)

will have to make choices and usually sacrifice one criterion in order to achieve the other two. Before I get too far, the three criteria that all investments are measured by are 1) Safety, 2) Liquidity, and 3) Rate of Return.

* * *

Safety

Safety is the measure of how secure the investment is. Differing investments have differing levels of safety.

Savings accounts at your local FDIC insured bank are at the top end of the safety meter (for amounts of $100,000 or less unless structured properly to get more FDIC coverage). Insured through the Federal Deposit Insurance Corporation, the only way the money you put into a savings account can be lost is if the country is invaded and taken over. In fairness, I think we all would have bigger concerns than our savings account at that point. Further down on the risk scale are stocks. Purchasing a percentage of ownership in a company can potentially reap tremendous financial rewards, but the company can go bankrupt, thereby losing the investment. Again, every investment needs to measure up in some way to the safety test. It takes time and effort to accrue capital in which to invest. Wise investors want to make sure that the time and effort spent to accrue the capital will not be wasted by making an unsafe investment.

* * *

Liquidity

Liquidity is the measure of how accessible the capital invested is to the investor. Just as there are differing levels of safety between various investments, there are differing levels of liquidity. Again, a savings account at your local bank has tremendous liquidity. You simply need to go down to your local branch, or any of thousands of ATMs throughout the country, and make a withdrawal. Savings accounts, obviously, are high on the liquidity meter. Other investments are not as liquid. A prime example would be many retirement accounts like 401ks or IRAs. While it is still the investor's money, there are very specific legal conditions for when they can access their accounts. Further, there are stiff penalties for investors who withdraw their money early or for reasons other than those outlined by the ever changing tax code. Clearly, investment vehicles like these are not high up on the liquidity meter.

* * *

Rate of Return

The third criterion that investments need to measure against is their rate of return. This measure indicates how much growth the investment experiences each year. The goal of every investor is to maximize this rate of return in order to grow their wealth in the quickest amount of time. Stocks very often have a high rate of return. Almost everyone who is interested in finances has contemplated what the differences would be in their life had they invested a small sum in Microsoft stock at the beginning of that company's rise to fame and fortune. The stock market, historically speaking, has significantly outpaced inflation by providing a higher rate of return. However, a bank savings account, historically speaking, has NOT significantly outpaced inflation, often performing below a 2% rate of return. Bank savings accounts score very low on the rate of return meter.

* * *

Putting It All Together

While almost all financial professionals agree on these three criteria as measurements that investments must weigh themselves against, there is great debate over the order in which the three criteria take precedence.

With those three criteria in mind, every investor must examine the goals for their life in general and their investments in particular. If the particular investor is in their early 20s, just getting started in life, and planning to let their investment grow until retirement, they might consider rate of return most important and be willing to sacrifice a bit of safety. An older person, seeing retirement on the near horizon might be more concerned with the safety of his hard earned capital and would be willing to sacrifice a bit of the rate of return for a greater guarantee on his investment. Again, these are factors that have to be determined by each individual investor. However, every investor wants the greatest amount of safety, the most liquidity, and the greatest rate of return that they can find.

In specific regard to the strategies we have outlined over the course of this book, the equity using investor really only has 3 viable options available to them for investing the difference between mortgage payments. The first option would be certain specific mutual funds. The second option would be certain specific annuities. The third option would be investment grade insurance contracts. We'll examine all three investment vehicles in turn.

* * *

Saving the Difference with Mutual Funds

Mutual Funds are a popular form of retirement investment vehicle for many Americans. The concept is simple. A mutual fund is a type of collective investment. Rather than individually buying stocks, bonds, and other securities, investors in a mutual fund pool their money and allow a fund manager to allocate where the capital will be invested. The fund manager purchases stocks, bonds, and other securities in an attempt to realize capital gains and dividends. If he is successful, the gains are passed on to the fund share holders. If he is unsuccessful, the fund share holders may realize a loss and the value of their shares diminishes.

Many Americans invest in mutual funds. Mutual funds are very commonly offered as a part of an employee's company retirement savings program. Most Americans with a 401k or IRA are invested in mutual funds. Further, Americans tend to like mutual funds because they like the perceived comfort of knowing that there is a fund manager at the helm guiding their investment along.

To gauge whether or not mutual funds are an ideal investment vehicle to use with our equity strategies that we've outlined (saving the difference between mortgage payments) we need to look at them through the rubric of whether they are safe, liquid, and their rate of return.

Using the most common measuring rod for mutual funds (the S&P 500), we can see that many mutual funds are not particularly safe. Looking back at the performance of funds over the past 30 years, there have been many years where funds have done wonderfully, but there have been years where they have not performed well. Safety is paramount for the home equity investor. With one's home equity being used as capital, risky losses cannot be tolerated. So, if one still opted for mutual funds as an equity investor, they would have to choose one of the more conservative funds. However, there will still not be a guarantee against a loss in most every mutual fund.

Another downside occurs at the withdrawal stage of retirement using 401k plans or IRAs. At 70 ½ years of age, investors must begin to take out money or they are penalized by the government and the penalty is stiff! The government will assess a 50% federal penalty on the required withdrawal amount every year that the required amount is not withdrawn on time. So, for example, if you were required to start withdrawing $20,000 from your IRA and you did not, the government would levy a 50% penalty against you. You would have to pay the government $10,000 on money that may not have been needed, not to mention the taxes due on the original $20,000. All of this simply because you didn't want to withdraw it!

Another downside to mutual funds purchased outside of a 401k or IRA for the equity investor is the tax implications. Mutual funds have a whole host of tax issues. First, the capital gains realized inside the mutual funds are passed through to the investor to be included in their taxable income every year. Greater tax burden means less contribution towards retirement. Further, any dividends that the mutual fund receives from the underlying stocks are also taxable to the mutual fund investor.

* * *

Saving the Difference With Annuities

Another popular retirement investment vehicle for many Americans is fixed or indexed annuities. An annuity basically is an investment contract with an insurance company.

Annuities are popular with Americans for several reasons. First, they can provide a stream of income during retirement that will never run out. The habit of receiving a steady paycheck throughout one's life is a hard habit to break. When chosen, an annuity continues that type of structure with steady payments month after month. Second, Americans like them because they are very safe. In fact, you can't lose money due to the stock market in a fixed or indexed annuity. In a fixed annuity your contract guarantees a certain rate of return. Third, the interest an annuity earns grows tax deferred. This eliminates a huge downside that mutual funds had.

With all these things going for them, it's no wonder that annuities are popular. However, there are downsides. The biggest downside rests in the lack of liquidity offered with annuities. Designed as an investment vehicle to provide income during a person's retirement, there is an early withdrawal penalty of 10% levied by the federal tax code for withdrawing money before age 59 ½. In fact, many states also impose a penalty on early withdrawals as well. For investors who are years away from retirement, annuities do not pass the liquidity test.

Another downside is that the money an annuity earns is taxed upon withdrawal at the investor's ordinary income level. As we've already discussed, the likelihood that a person entering retirement will be in a lower tax bracket is not particularly high. Upon withdrawal after age 59 ½, the gain is dispersed from the annuity before your cost basis (the original dollars you put into the annuity) and is taxed as ordinary income. The taxation on the gains made inside the annuity is referred to as LIFO taxation (last in, first out). Again, in our opinion, fixed and indexed annuities, while providing greater safety than mutual funds, still do not offer the best investment vehicle for home equity investors especially for younger investors. Home equity investors who are in their mid to later 50's and up might find this the proper vehicle.

* * *

Investment Grade Insurance Contracts

If there was a way to grow your money tax free, pull your money out of the investment tax free, have no penalties for accessing your money before age 59 ½, whatsoever, and the investor received stock market returns without ever being in danger of losing money in the stock market, that would be the ideal investment not just for home equity dollars, but every dollar you have to invest period. Well I'm sad to say that this mythical dream investment doesn't exist. But there is a vehicle that is a close runner up.

An investment grade insurance contract allows the monies invested to grow on a tax deferred basis. There is the potential to pull the money out of the contract without having to pay taxes on the interest earned. The amount of interest earned inside of the contract is linked to the stock market *but the money is not in the stock* market and therefore is not in danger of losing principal or interest gained due to stock market declines. What this means is that when an investment grade insurance contract is tied to the S&P 500 and the S&P 500 goes up, so does your money inside the contract. When the S&P 500 goes down your principal and gains cannot be taken away due to a market decline, there is just no interest earned for that period of time. In addition to the features briefly described above, there is a liquidity feature that is unique to this vehicle. There is access to some portion (and at times, the entire portion) of the cash inside of the contract.

When this vehicle is described to the astute investor, their first response is often one of confusion. The most general question is at the core of this confusion. "I've been investing for a while, how come I've never heard of this vehicle before?" We have been to seminars conducted by our peers regarding this vehicle and at times we have felt like their seminar presentation had the look and feel of a "smoke and mirrors" routine. The term Investment Grade

Insurance Contract is used because calling this vehicle by its legal name might turn part of the viewing audience off.

If you have come with us this far in the book, we ask you to go just a little further. What is being described as an Investment Grade Insurance Contract is really an Indexed Universal Life Insurance Policy.

While not nearly as popular or well known as mutual funds or annuities, the indexed universal life insurance policy (forthwith IUL policy) best meets the criteria we've established for a good investment.

First, a little trip down memory lane is in order. If you are old enough to be thinking about retirement then you are old enough to remember a very popular series of commercials from the late 1970s/early 1980s. Several variations of the commercial ran, but they all had the same theme. In the commercial the camera would pan around a crowded room of people, often a noisy cocktail party, at which point it would zoom in on a pair of young professionals chatting. Amidst the din of the party and the numerous conversations, one of the young professionals would utter the phrase, "Well, my broker is E.F. Hutton and..." However, before the young professional could complete his statement the music would stop, other conversations ceased, and people around the room would lean in to hear what was being discussed. The catch phrase for E.F. Hutton was then announced in a deep, resonant voice, "When E.F. Hutton talks, people listen." Whether or not that was the case, E.F. Hutton was, for several decades, one of the largest brokerage firms in the United States. The point of our little glimpse of nostalgia is that while most Americans remember that commercial and the name E.F. Hutton, most Americans were (and still are) entirely unaware of how that company revolutionized the investment industry through the use of life insurance.

Back in 1979, E.F. Hutton (then Life Insurance Company of California) discovered that life insurance had very special provisions given to it in the IRS Tax Code. Namely, life insurance policies allowed for tax deferred growth of the money invested, and had the potential for tax-free income during the withdrawal period. Further, it allowed for an income tax free transfer upon the death of the insured. This revelation solved nearly all of the tax implications that frustrated investors as they planned, saved, and experienced retirement.

E.F. Hutton knew that they had a great idea. Because of the tremendous tax advantages available through life insurance, they knew that life insurance had the potential to make a great vehicle for supplemental retirement income. At this point they developed the Universal Life Insurance policy. Sophisticated investors flocked to the policies. Recognizing the tax benefits, investors stuffed hundreds of thousands, sometimes even millions into the policies. The only thing that investors needed to do at that time to gain the tax advantages was prove that they were buying life insurance. So, what often happened was that investors would purchase $10,000 worth of insurance and then dump hundreds of thousands of dollars into the account because originally there was no limit to the amount that one could put into the policies.

The IRS realized fairly quickly that this strategy could cost the government coffers a lot if people caught on to the strategy. To try and stop the practice the IRS fought these new contracts through the courts and through the passage of new laws by Congress. They realized that these life insurance contracts, if properly structured, would behave very much like an investment but have the tax treatment of life insurance.

Under sections 7702 and 72(e) of the Internal Revenue Code, life insurance is allowed to accumulate tax deferred and the cash values of the policy are allowed to be withdrawn tax free when a policy loan is utilized (more on this later). The biggest kicker for life insurance is that under section 101 of the tax code, death benefits are paid to the beneficiary income tax free (the death benefit may still be counted when determining estate taxes). So when E.F. Hutton created this super product under the laws of life insurance, it only took a few years for congress to respond.

Congress changed the tax laws regarding life insurance not once, but three times starting in 1982, then in 1984 and concluding in 1988. These laws are known as the TEFRA Act of 1982, The DEFRA Act of 1984, and the TAMRA Act of 1988. These new regulations basically changed the way that the life insurance policies could be funded but not how they worked. There were now limitations on how much money could be put into the policy based upon the amount of insurance purchased (in essence, no more $10,000 life insurance policies to stash away $500,000 in savings). It also restricted how fast you could fund the policy by requiring you to spread it out over 4 or 5 years for a life insurance product using the framework of a universal life policy or 7 years for a life insurance product using the framework of a whole life policy. However, the IRS still did not take away the tax deferred growth and the potential tax free income provisions of the policy. Many of our nation's wealthiest people today are still using universal life insurance policies to build their wealth and secure their wealth.

With our little history lesson completed, let's examine how Indexed Universal Life Insurance measures up with our criteria for good investments.

Our first criterion is safety. We do not want to risk the equity in our house on an unsafe investment. Safety is a huge concern for home equity investors. However, Indexed Universal Life Insurance has a safety element to it. Here is how it works. The term indexed refers to the fact that these policies are tied to a financial index like the S&P 500, NASDAQ, Russell 2000, Dow Jones, etc. When money is invested into one of these indexed policies, the rate of return will be based on the index that the policy is tied to. One of the aspects of these policies is how they are designed to maximize investment safety. All of these policies are guaranteed against the loss of principal due to market performance of the linked index. In fact, companies guarantee some gain over a specified period of time. An example might be that Company A guarantees a minimum 1% rate of return annually, even if the index that the policy is tied to has recorded a loss. While 1% interest is not an exciting rate of return, it is amazing considering that people investing on the same index, but not in indexed policies, would have lost a bundle if the index declined. Company B might offer a guarantee of 2% over a 5 year period. In other words, if the index the policy is linked to has a declining 5 year period and the policy holder didn't at least earn 2% over that 5 year period, the insurance company will go back and credit 2% per year retroactively. Company C & D might have a different method for offering some sort of guaranteed growth.

An important note to make is that while your downside potential in the market is eliminated, your upside potential in the market is capped. An example for clarity is in order.

Tony decides to buy a commonly offered indexed universal life insurance policy that is offering an annual floor of 1% and a ceiling cap rate of 12% tied to the S&P 500 index. The first year that Tony has his policy the S&P takes a nose dive and loses 9%. While this is terrible, Tony still would earn 1% in his policy (the policy has a 1% floor). Disappointed with the poor performance, Tony hopes for a better year next year. His fortunes change and next year the S&P is up gaining 8%! Tony would realize an 8% gain on his investment. Next year, the S&P has a banner year and soars up by 16%! At this point Tony earns 12% on his investment (his ceiling is 12%). The indexed universal life insurance policy has allowed Tony to avoid the disastrous year where it lost 9% and to enjoy the up years and only miss out on part of the boom. This degree of safety is a key feature of the indexed universal life insurance policy.

The next criterion for a good investment is liquidity. Just as in the safety category, the indexed universal life insurance policy holds up well in the liquidity department. Unlike IRAs, 401k plans, or annuities that have penalties for non-approved early withdrawals, there are several ways to access ones money in an IUL policy without having to pay income tax.

The first way to access your money without having to pay income tax is to simply withdraw the money you have put into the policy. As long as the amount does not exceed what you have put into the policy, no income tax is due. This money is what is known as the "cost basis". The only caveat to be aware of is that if one withdraws money in excess of what they have put into their policy then they will have to pay income tax on that money.

The second way to access your money without paying income tax is to withdraw money in the form of a policy loan. At this point many people ask a very good question- "Why would I want to borrow my own money?" The answer simply put is because *loans are not taxable*. Think about it. You don't have to pay taxes on the loan for your house (Some of you are thinking, "I pay property tax!" Property tax is not a tax on your home loan; it is a tax on the value of your property.). You don't have to pay taxes on the loan you got for your car. Additionally, you will not have to pay taxes on a loan from your own insurance policy. Here's an illustration to demonstrate how this works.

Imagine 20 years after you bought your policy your kids are ready to enter college or you want to put in a pool in the backyard or envision any other big ticket item that you fancy. The first thing you are going to have to do is figure out how to finance it. You could take out an equity line of credit and pay the bank for allowing you to access your equity. Or, since you have your indexed universal life insurance policy, you can borrow against that. All you would have to do to secure the loan is call the insurance company and take a policy loan for $100,000 (assuming you have $100,000 to access from your policy). There are no credit approval forms or any qualifying hoops to jump through because you are borrowing against your existing policy. The insurance company will then write you a check for $100,000 out of their company assets, not your own money. Then they reach into your account and pull out $100,000 to hold as collateral for this loan (hence you must have more than $100,000 in your policy). To prove to the IRS that this is in fact a loan and not a withdrawal, the insurance company has to charge you an interest rate to prove that it's a loan. So, the insurance company will charge you an interest rate of let's say 5% (this rate varies by company). However, they then credit the $100,000 they are holding as collateral for your loan 5% interest. This is what is called a net-zero or wash loan. The percentage they charge you is the same as the percentage they credit you. You have now taken out a $100,000 without having to pay taxes on it! A final benefit to this loan is that you do not need to make payments on the loan. This is because the insurance company already has your $100,000 from your policy as collateral. Technically, the loan will be paid back at the time of your death (the loan amount will simply be subtracted from the existing policy value, reducing the death benefit, and the excess will be passed on to the beneficiary).

The final criterion that the indexed universal life insurance needs to meet is rate of return. These policies are indexed to varying financial markets and receive returns based on the returns of the market they are tied to. This being the case, the returns, historically have been lucrative. In fact, one of our favorite companies has a rate of return average of over 9% for the past 22 years. This rate is significantly higher than fixed annuities and even many mutual funds. Further, the rate is not only higher, it is accomplished while avoiding all of the losses and worry that comes with having investments directly invested in the stock market.

The key to using an indexed universal life policy for the accumulation of cash and the tax favored withdrawals comes down to the proper structuring of the policy. To underscore yet again, before implementing this or any other strategy discussed in this book, consult your tax, legal and/or financial professional first. Because of the volume of people that come through our offices, we see how this strategy can be used to greatly aide in reaching ones financial goals, and we have also seen how this strategy can be improperly implemented only to have it self-destruct. One of the reasons we created the Certified Mortgage Investment Advisor designation was so that we could ensure the training of mortgage, financial, and insurance professionals in regards to all of the concepts from this book.

If an indexed universal life policy is not set up and funded properly, three potentially devastating conditions can happen. The tax free loans will no longer be available to the policy owner, the internal fees can eat up the policy's cash, and all the tax free loans can become taxable.

Earlier in this chapter, it was mentioned that you must fund a policy over a 4 to 5 year term. If, for instance, it was the desire of a homeowner to take $100,000 from their home's equity and $50,000 from their savings and fund a IUL policy with that, if those monies were placed into the policy the first year you would have what is referred to as a Modified Endowment Contract (or MEC for short). A MEC contract does not enjoy the benefits when it comes to life insurance. Withdrawals and loans of gains do not come out tax free and they cannot be made prior to 59 ½ without incurring a 10% federal penalty, much like on a 401k or IRA. There are specific guidelines that a policy holder must follow when building a policy, but all of these guidelines revolve around the amount of money that is desired to be put in. These guidelines change for each policy holder based on the insured's age, health rating, and gender. To aide the professional that is building these policies, most insurance companies provide licensed agents' software that aids the agent in building the policy that keeps them in compliance with the laws governing the proper structure of their specific company products.

Another interesting fact regarding these policies is that you can have more than one. Often times people tell us of their concern that they will open a contract that can't hold enough money. They feel that in the future they will be able to put in more money than they currently have access to. The good news is that there is no federal limit on the number of contracts one is eligible to open. The bad news in that one must qualify with the insurance company to open a new contract. Always remember that these contracts are life insurance. If health no longer permits, an insurance company will not give a policy to someone just because they desire to put money aside. It is during these times that the idea of a surrogate is introduced. Often times someone comes to us whose health will not allow them to qualify for life insurance. It is under these circumstances that we introduce the surrogate concept.

With the surrogate concept, the policy owner is the one that controls the policy and the access to the cash inside. They are the one that benefits from the tax deferral of a policy and the tax free withdrawals and loans. The surrogate is someone the policy holder has a financial interest in. It can be a spouse, a child, grandchild, or some other relationship.

Another major concern when building a policy is that the fees of the policy can diminish the cash inside the policy. This typically happens when it is not structured properly. Let's say a family wants their contract to hold $100,000 from equity they just separated from their home and the $50,000 from their savings. After deciding how much they want to put into their contract, they call their insurance agent who has helped them for years. The insurance agent, who has been in the business for many years, is happy to provide the family with another life insurance policy. Unfortunately, while the agent's skills at selling life insurance are adequate for a typical life insurance policy, his knowledge of how to properly build this type of policy is lacking. Because it is not built correctly, the policy is designed to hold $250,000.

The problem that arises is that because the policy was built to hold more money than the family is going to put in the policy, the policy fees and expenses are greater than they need or should be. The fees charged by the insurance company are based on the life insurance required to put in $250,000 not the $150,000 the family actually plans to put in. This will have a dramatic effect on the accumulation of cash value in the policy. What the agent should have done was build the policy to only hold the total amount of money that is going to be placed in the contract, be it over 4 years, 5 years or even 11 years. The goal is to have what is referred to as a Maximum Funded Contract.

Lastly, we must caution you, there is another downside to this strategy. It is called an over-loan. What allows this money to be tax free when taken as a policy loan is because it is being given to you from a life insurance product. If you close the policy (known as surrendering) or you lapse the policy (this happens when there is no longer enough money in the policy to pay the cost of insurance for the death benefit), those loans may become taxable. Remember, this is not a short term vehicle. This is a long term vehicle. We recommend that when you are evaluating IUL insurance companies you look for what is called an over-loan protection feature. These protection features (often come as riders on the policy with no fee until they are used) work differently with each company that offers them, but how many of them typically work is if you are over 75 years of age and your policy is going to lapse due to borrowing too much money from it and it has been in place for a number of years, the policy will convert to a "paid up" policy. No more cost of insurance for the death benefit, so now it doesn't lapse and the disaster has been averted.

Some people have had bad experiences with Universal Life policies. In most cases that is because they had purchased the policy as a form of death insurance. That is not what we are trying to accomplish. We are looking to use a Universal Life policy (specifically an Indexed Universal Life policy) as a vehicle that we can stuff full of cash, as much as the IRS allows, and which will provide us with the safety, liquidity, and a rate of return that we can feel secure about. In addition, when the policy is structured correctly, we receive tax advantages in the accumulation, withdrawal, and transfer periods of retirement planning

* * *

How Do They Do That?

At one of our Equity Wealth Seminars a guest from the audience came up afterwards and inquired as to what would happen if the stock market continued to crash year after year and the insurance companies were forced to provide the guarantee that the policy holder could not lose money due to stock market decline. Would that force the insurance companies to go out of business?

Interestingly enough, it has been estimated that 84% of agents licensed to offer indexed universal life and indexed annuities do not know how the insurance companies are able to guarantee their policy holders will not lose money due to the stock market declines. Most agents explain that the reason the insurance company can guarantee no loss in the indexed account is because they have a cap or ceiling on how well your investment can do. When the market does better than the cap, they get to keep that money for themselves. Indeed when I first entered the financial planning industry, my supervisor gave me this exact explanation. It sounds logical, but nothing could be further from the truth.

An Indexed Universal Life policy is built on the framework of a Universal Life policy. Because of that, it is important to understand the basics of a straight UL policy. For every dollar the insurance company receives for a UL policy, the insurance company buys bonds. Typically they are high-grade bonds. These bonds pay interest to the insurance company. The company uses this interest to pay commissions to the agent, profit for the company, and the interest on the money inside of the UL contract to the policy holder.

An Indexed Universal Life works similarly behind the scenes. The money the insurance company receives from the policy owner (this money is referred to as premiums) goes to buy these same high-grade bonds. The interest paid by the bonds is used to pay commissions to the agent, provide the company with a profit source, and instead of paying interest to the policy holder on the money inside of the IUL contract, a smaller portion is used to provide the guaranteed growth rate and the rest is used to buy Call Options on the financial index the IUL policy is tied to.

When many people hear the term Options, their first instinct is to assume risk is involved. What they are thinking about is Option Trading and that is not what the insurance companies are doing. Call Options are the right, not the obligation, to buy the underlying security. If the market is up at the end of the Option period (typically 12 months later, but sometimes 24 months later) the Option is exercised and the profits flow back to the insurance company and then to the policy holder to give them the profit promised on the policy. If the market is down at the end of the Option period the Option expires worthless so no money is credited to the policy. In a very real sense, the insurance company is not concerned with the performance of the stock markets. Up or down, there is no direct effect on the insurance company. The insurance company prefers it when the markets end high because that means more people will want to buy their products.

The companies that have the higher cap rates and participation rates are putting more money toward the purchase of Options and less money to the company's bottom line and the agent's commissions. Because the cost of the Options can go up and down, the insurance company will need to raise or lower the cap rates and participation rates on the policies as the need demands.

Each insurance company has different indexing strategies. The basic strategy is the strategy that has already been explained. It is referred to as a "cap focus". If your policy gives you a 12% cap with 100% participation and the market does 15%, you will earn 12% (due to the cap) on your money. Let us say that another strategy being offered by the company is a "participation focus" option. It might look different than the cap focus strategy. If your policy gives you no cap with a 75% participation and the market does 15%, you would receive 11.25% (due to the participation rate of 75%). On the surface, one strategy might look better than the other, but it is impossible to know with any degree of certainty which one is going to perform better. Some sound advice would be to split your money up over several strategies as most companies that offer more than one strategy will allow you to do so.

Seeking the counsel of a professional specifically trained to handle such policies is advised.

* * *

The Variable Loan

There is yet another way to access funds in an Indexed Universal Life policy. While somewhat abstract, if understood it can be one of the most powerful financial planning techniques available to investors today! It is a different type of policy loan. It works the same way as the traditional policy loan that was previously described with just a slight difference. That difference can have an amazing result!

Let's flash forward again 15 years from when you bought your policy. You are now ready to start taking some supplemental retirement income. You call up the company and start a policy loan for $50,000. Instead of electing the net-zero loan, you elect the "variable" loan. The way the variable loan works is this: instead of charging a fixed interest rate on the money borrowed, they charge a rate based on (most often) the Moody Corporate Bond Index (at the time of this writing it is about 5.8%). Then your $50,000 is not removed from your account. It is allowed to stay in the indexed account earning whatever the account earns. The average over the last 22 years with one of the major companies is 8.7%. If it earns 8.9% and it costs you 5.8% then that means you made 2.9% on money that you have already spent! The 20 year history between the Moody Corporate Bond Index and the S&P 500 (factoring in a 12% cap rate with 100% participation) is around 1 to 2%. At the time of this writing, the same company used above as an example is consistently hitting the 12% cap for the policy holder while the Moody Corporate Bond Index is around 5.8%. That is a difference of over 6% on money already taken from the policy. However, it is extremely important to realize that some years you will earn less than what you pay. Other years you will earn much more than what you paid in interest. For most companies that offer this strategy you will have the option of using the variable loan or the net zero loan when you finally decide to take money from the policy. Some insurance companies will even allow the investor to switch between the variable loan option and the net-zero loan option on an annual basis at the policy anniversary. This gives the policy owner even greater flexibility with their policy. The long term history on this strategy is impressive.

* * *

Based on the criteria of a good investment (safety, liquidity, and rate of return) it is our opinion that the indexed universal life insurance may be the best option available to the equity investor. Consulting a trained professional can help you decide if it is the best option for you and your family.

Where to Put the Extra Money - 161

* * *

In closing, let's examine a few examples on the following pages:

162 - The New Mortgage Investment Advisor

This illustration is based on Phillip Anderson from chapter 6. Since there are IRS limits on how quickly the savings can be placed in the IUL policy, we showed the $106,312.40, from the Secured Option ARM example, invested evenly over the first 5 years. A 34.3% tax bracket is used. The Certificate of Deposit is taxed as earned, the annuity is growing tax deferred until withdrawals are made and then it is taxed as ordinary income. The IRA is for demonstration only. IRAs cannot be funded at $21,362 per year under the current tax code. The IRA is taxed as ordinary income when withdrawals are made. There are no taxes due on the IUL distributions since the withdrawals are up to the cost basis and then the loan provision of the insurance contract is being used after that. (See page 121 for source numbers)

	Tax Type	Interest Rate	Management Fee	Premature Dist. Tax	Sales Charge
Certificate of Deposit	Taxable	6.00%	0.00%	0.00%	0.00%
Annuity	Deferred	7.00%	0.00%	10.00%	0.00%
IRA/401(k)	Deferred	9.00%	1.00%	10.00%	0.00%
Indexed Universal Life Insurance	Tax Advantaged	8.00%			

Withdrawals to Cost Basis and then Net-Zero Loan Option.

			After Tax Values			Insurance Values		
Age	Contribution (Premium)	After Tax amount of Withdrawal (Loan)	Certificate of Deposit	Annuity	IRA	Cash Value	Surrender Value	Death Benefit
35	$21,362	$0	$22,205	$22,858	$23,071	$19,149	$11,793	$720,474
36	$21,362	$0	$45,284	$47,316	$47,989	$39,768	$28,600	$720,474
37	$21,362	$0	$69,274	$73,486	$74,899	$61,973	$52,045	$720,474
38	$21,362	$0	$94,210	$101,488	$103,963	$85,905	$77,223	$720,474
39	$21,362	$0	$120,128	$131,450	$135,351	$111,705	$104,263	$720,474
40	$0	$0	$124,863	$140,651	$146,179	$117,592	$111,389	$720,474
41	$0	$0	$129,785	$150,497	$157,874	$123,896	$118,932	$720,474
42	$0	$0	$134,902	$161,031	$170,503	$130,658	$126,934	$720,474
43	$0	$0	$140,219	$172,304	$184,144	$137,907	$135,428	$720,474
44	$0	$0	$145,747	$184,365	$198,875	$147,430	$146,190	$720,474
45	$0	$0	$151,492	$197,270	$214,785	$159,280	$159,280	$720,474
46	$0	$0	$157,464	$211,079	$231,968	$172,124	$172,124	$720,474
47	$0	$0	$163,671	$225,855	$250,526	$186,025	$186,025	$720,474
48	$0	$0	$170,123	$241,665	$270,568	$201,097	$201,097	$720,474
49	$0	$0	$176,829	$258,581	$292,213	$217,505	$217,505	$720,474
50	$0	$0	$183,800	$276,682	$315,590	$235,356	$235,356	$720,474
51	$0	$0	$191,045	$296,050	$340,837	$254,776	$254,776	$720,474
52	$0	$0	$198,576	$316,773	$368,104	$275,920	$275,920	$720,474
53	$0	$0	$206,404	$338,947	$397,553	$298,947	$298,947	$720,474
54	$0	$0	$214,541	$362,673	$429,357	$324,018	$324,018	$720,474
55	$0	$0	$222,998	$388,061	$463,705	$351,350	$351,350	$720,474
56	$0	$0	$231,789	$415,225	$500,802	$381,167	$381,167	$720,474
57	$0	$0	$240,926	$444,291	$540,866	$413,714	$413,714	$720,474

Where to Put the Extra Money - 163

Age								
58	$0	$0	$250,423	$475,391	$584,135	$449,347	$449,347	$720,474
59	$0	$0	$260,295	$508,668	$630,866	$488,372	$488,372	$720,474
60	$0	$0	$270,555	$544,275	$681,335	$531,062	$531,062	$720,474
61	$0	$0	$281,221	$582,374	$735,842	$577,910	$577,910	$739,725
62	$0	$0	$292,306	$623,141	$794,709	$629,102	$629,102	$792,669
63	$0	$0	$303,829	$666,760	$858,286	$684,863	$684,863	$849,230
64	$0	$0	$315,806	$713,434	$926,949	$745,620	$745,620	$909,657
65	$0	-$60,188	$265,695	$665,484	$902,300	$746,199	$746,199	$895,439
66	$0	-$60,188	$213,608	$614,178	$875,680	$761,373	$746,806	$891,467
67	$0	-$60,188	$159,467	$559,281	$846,930	$827,245	$747,258	$896,162
68	$0	-$60,188	$103,193	$500,541	$815,879	$897,484	$747,497	$900,069
69	$0	-$60,188	$44,700	$437,689	$782,345	$972,390	$747,502	$903,084
70	$0	-$60,188	$0	$370,437	$746,128	$1,052,249	$747,217	$905,055
71	$0	-$60,188	$0	$298,478	$707,014	$1,137,621	$746,836	$894,727
72	$0	-$60,188	$0	$221,482	$664,770	$1,228,960	$746,419	$881,605
73	$0	-$60,188	$0	$139,096	$619,147	$1,326,788	$746,069	$865,480
74	$0	-$60,188	$0	$50,943	$569,874	$1,431,706	$745,934	$846,154
75	$0	-$60,188	$0	$0	$516,659	$1,544,418	$746,242	$823,462
76	$0	-$60,188	$0	$0	$459,188	$1,664,610	$746,160	$829,390
77	$0	-$60,188	$0	$0	$397,118	$1,792,694	$745,552	$835,186
78	$0	-$60,188	$0	$0	$330,083	$1,929,114	$744,271	$840,726
79	$0	-$60,188	$0	$0	$257,685	$2,074,317	$742,133	$845,849
80	$0	-$60,188	$0	$0	$179,495	$2,228,782	$738,944	$850,383
81	$0	-$60,188	$0	$0	$95,050	$2,392,999	$734,471	$854,121
82	$0	-$60,188	$0	$0	$3,849	$2,567,515	$728,489	$856,865
83	$0	-$60,188	$0	$0	$0	$2,752,873	$720,715	$858,358
84	$0	-$60,188	$0	$0	$0	$2,949,515	$710,703	$858,179
85	$0	-$60,188	$0	$0	$0	$3,157,833	$697,904	$855,796
86	$0	-$60,188	$0	$0	$0	$3,378,124	$681,599	$850,505
87	$0	-$60,188	$0	$0	$0	$3,610,812	$661,129	$841,670
88	$0	-$60,188	$0	$0	$0	$3,856,391	$635,829	$828,648
89	$0	-$60,188	$0	$0	$0	$4,115,412	$605,010	$810,780
90	$0	-$60,188	$0	$0	$0	$4,388,384	$567,852	$787,271
91	$0	-$60,188	$0	$0	$0	$4,681,743	$529,372	$716,642
92	$0	-$60,188	$0	$0	$0	$4,998,189	$490,752	$640,697
93	$0	-$60,188	$0	$0	$0	$5,340,874	$453,515	$560,332
94	$0	-$60,188	$0	$0	$0	$5,714,166	$420,290	$477,432
95	$0	-$60,188	$0	$0	$0	$6,111,495	$382,647	$443,761
96	$0	-$60,188	$0	$0	$0	$6,534,459	$340,190	$405,535
97	$0	-$60,188	$0	$0	$0	$6,985,032	$292,764	$362,614
98	$0	-$60,188	$0	$0	$0	$7,464,824	$239,695	$314,344

(Figure 7.1 ~ This illustrates the non-guaranteed values for all years. Actual results will be lower or higher.)

The total funds committed to this comparison were $106,312 deposited over a 5 year period. The Amount withdrawn from the Indexed Universal Life over 33 years is $1,986,204 with $239,695 still left in the policy. The CD ran out of money at age 70, the annuity at age 75 and the IRA at age 83.

164 - The New Mortgage Investment Advisor

This illustration is based on Phillip Anderson from chapter 6. Since there are IRS limits on how quickly the savings can be placed in the IUL policy, we showed the $106,812.40, from the Secured Option ARM example, invested evenly over the first 5 years. A 34.3% tax bracket is used. The Certificate of Deposit is taxed as earned, the annuity is growing tax deferred until withdrawals are made and then it is taxed as ordinary income. The IRA is for demonstration only. IRAs cannot be funded at $21,362 per year under the current tax code. The IRA is taxed as ordinary income when withdrawals are made. There are no taxes due on the IUL distributions since the withdrawals are using the variable loan feature with a 1% arbitrage. (See page 121 for source numbers.)

	Tax Type	Interest Rate	Management Fee	Premature Dist. Tax	Sales Charge
Certificate of Deposit	Taxable	6.00%	0.00%	0.00%	0.00%
Annuity	Deferred	7.00%	0.00%	10.00%	0.00%
IRA/401(k)	Deferred	9.00%	1.00%	10.00%	0.00%
Indexed Universal Life Insurance	Tax Advantaged	8.00%			

Withdrawals are Done with the Variable Loan Option at 1% Arbitrage.

Age	Contribution (Premium)	After Tax Amount of Withdrawal (Loan)	Certificate of Deposit	Annuity	IRA	Cash Value	Surrender Value	Death Benefit
35	$21,362	$0	$22,205	$22,858	$23,071	$19,149	$11,793	$720,474
36	$21,362	$0	$45,284	$47,316	$47,989	$39,768	$28,600	$720,474
37	$21,362	$0	$69,274	$73,486	$74,899	$61,973	$52,045	$720,474
38	$21,362	$0	$94,210	$101,488	$103,963	$85,905	$77,223	$720,474
39	$21,362	$0	$120,128	$131,450	$135,351	$111,705	$104,263	$720,474
40	$0	$0	$124,863	$140,651	$146,179	$117,592	$111,389	$720,474
41	$0	$0	$129,785	$150,497	$157,874	$123,896	$118,932	$720,474
42	$0	$0	$134,902	$161,031	$170,503	$130,658	$126,934	$720,474
43	$0	$0	$140,219	$172,304	$184,144	$137,907	$135,428	$720,474
44	$0	$0	$145,747	$184,365	$198,875	$147,430	$146,190	$720,474
45	$0	$0	$151,492	$197,270	$214,785	$159,280	$159,280	$720,474
46	$0	$0	$157,464	$211,079	$231,968	$172,124	$172,124	$720,474
47	$0	$0	$163,671	$225,855	$250,526	$186,025	$186,025	$720,474
48	$0	$0	$170,123	$241,665	$270,568	$201,097	$201,097	$720,474
49	$0	$0	$176,829	$258,581	$292,213	$217,505	$217,505	$720,474
50	$0	$0	$183,800	$276,682	$315,590	$235,356	$235,356	$720,474
51	$0	$0	$191,045	$296,050	$340,837	$254,776	$254,776	$720,474
52	$0	$0	$198,576	$316,773	$368,104	$275,920	$275,920	$720,474
53	$0	$0	$206,404	$338,947	$397,553	$298,947	$298,947	$720,474
54	$0	$0	$214,541	$362,673	$429,357	$324,018	$324,018	$720,474
55	$0	$0	$222,998	$388,061	$463,705	$351,350	$351,350	$720,474
56	$0	$0	$231,789	$415,225	$500,802	$381,167	$381,167	$720,474

Where to Put the Extra Money - 165

Age								
57	$0	$0	$240,926	$444,291	$540,866	$413,714	$413,714	$720,474
58	$0	$0	$250,423	$475,391	$584,135	$449,347	$449,347	$720,474
59	$0	$0	$260,295	$508,668	$630,866	$488,372	$488,372	$720,474
60	$0	$0	$270,555	$544,275	$681,335	$531,062	$531,062	$720,474
61	$0	$0	$281,221	$582,374	$735,842	$577,910	$577,910	$739,725
62	$0	$0	$292,306	$623,141	$794,709	$629,102	$629,102	$792,669
63	$0	$0	$303,829	$666,760	$858,286	$684,863	$684,863	$849,230
64	$0	$0	$315,806	$713,434	$926,949	$745,620	$745,620	$909,657
65	$0	$-91,805	$232,831	$614,062	$850,398	$811,847	$713,616	$875,985
66	$0	$-91,805	$146,586	$507,735	$767,723	$883,957	$680,618	$848,570
67	$0	$-91,805	$56,940	$393,965	$678,433	$962,488	$646,684	$819,932
68	$0	$-91,805	$0	$272,231	$582,001	$1,048,012	$611,870	$790,033
69	$0	$-91,805	$0	$141,975	$477,854	$1,141,173	$576,270	$758,858
70	$0	$-91,805	$0	$2,602	$365,375	$1,242,632	$539,955	$726,350
71	$0	$-91,805	$0	$0	$243,898	$1,353,422	$503,326	$679,271
72	$0	$-91,805	$0	$0	$112,703	$1,474,490	$466,656	$628,849
73	$0	$-91,805	$0	$0	$0	$1,606,919	$430,305	$574,928
74	$0	$-91,805	$0	$0	$0	$1,751,945	$394,736	$517,373
75	$0	$-91,805	$0	$0	$0	$1,911,000	$360,556	$456,106
76	$0	$-91,805	$0	$0	$0	$2,084,288	$327,081	$431,296
77	$0	$-91,805	$0	$0	$0	$2,272,985	$294,542	$408,192
78	$0	$-91,805	$0	$0	$0	$2,478,377	$263,212	$387,131
79	$0	$-91,805	$0	$0	$0	$2,701,832	$233,374	$368,466
80	$0	$-91,805	$0	$0	$0	$2,944,842	$205,360	$352,602
81	$0	$-91,805	$0	$0	$0	$3,209,006	$179,530	$339,980
82	$0	$-91,805	$0	$0	$0	$3,496,099	$156,328	$331,133
83	$0	$-91,805	$0	$0	$0	$3,807,998	$136,212	$326,612
84	$0	$-91,805	$0	$0	$0	$4,146,555	$119,513	$326,840
85	$0	$-91,805	$0	$0	$0	$4,513,670	$106,503	$332,187
86	$0	$-91,805	$0	$0	$0	$4,911,219	$97,319	$342,880
87	$0	$-91,805	$0	$0	$0	$5,341,402	$92,298	$359,368
88	$0	$-91,805	$0	$0	$0	$5,806,675	$91,902	$382,236
89	$0	$-91,805	$0	$0	$0	$6,309,755	$96,717	$412,204
90	$0	$-91,805	$0	$0	$0	$6,853,471	$107,289	$449,962
91	$0	$-91,805	$0	$0	$0	$7,450,431	$133,784	$431,802
92	$0	$-91,805	$0	$0	$0	$8,107,844	$180,801	$424,037
93	$0	$-91,805	$0	$0	$0	$8,834,103	$253,935	$430,618
94	$0	$-91,805	$0	$0	$0	$9,640,204	$361,194	$457,596
95	$0	$-91,805	$0	$0	$0	$10,518,684	$491,911	$597,098
96	$0	$-91,805	$0	$0	$0	$11,476,204	$649,326	$764,088
97	$0	$-91,805	$0	$0	$0	$12,520,543	$837,553	$962,758
98	$0	$-91,805	$0	$0	$0	$13,659,306	$1,060,274	$1,196,867

Figure 7.2 ~ This illustrates the non-guaranteed values for all years. Actual results will be lower or higher.)

The total funds committed to this comparison were $106,812 deposited over a 5 year period. The Amount withdrawn from the Indexed Universal Life over 33 years is $3,029,565 with $1,060,274 still left in the policy. The CD ran out of money at age 68, the annuity at age 71 and the IRA at age 73.

166 - The New Mortgage Investment Advisor

This illustration is based on a 45 year old male withdrawing $300,000 of equity for supplemental retirement income. A 34.3% tax bracket is used. The Certificate of Deposit is taxed as earned, the annuity is growing tax deferred until withdrawals are made and then it is taxed as ordinary income. The IRA is for demonstration only. IRAs cannot be funded at $60,000 per year under the current tax code. The IRA is taxed as ordinary income when withdrawals are made. There are no taxes due on the IUL distributions since the withdrawals are up to the cost basis and then the loan provision of the insurance contract is being used after that.

	Tax Type	Interest Rate	Management Fee	Premature Dist. Tax	Sales Charge
Certificate of Deposit	Taxable	6.00%	0.00%	0.00%	0.00%
Annuity	Deferred	7.00%	0.00%	10.00%	0.00%
IRA/401(k)	Deferred	9.00%	1.00%	10.00%	0.00%
Indexed Universal Life Insurance	Tax Advantaged	8.00%			

Withdrawals to Cost Basis and then Net-Zero Loan Option.

Age	Contribution (Premium)	After Tax Amount of Withdrawal (Loan)	After Tax Values — Certificate of Deposit	Annuity	IRA	Insurance Values — Cash Value	Surrender Value	Death Benefit
45	$60,000	$0	$62,365	$64,200	$64,800	$53,758	$31,978	$1,295,668
46	$60,000	$0	$127,189	$132,894	$134,784	$111,562	$79,624	$1,295,668
47	$60,000	$0	$194,568	$206,397	$210,367	$173,800	$145,411	$1,295,668
48	$60,000	$0	$264,603	$285,044	$291,996	$240,855	$216,018	$1,295,668
49	$60,000	$0	$337,399	$369,197	$380,156	$313,111	$291,823	$1,295,668
50	$0	$0	$350,699	$395,041	$410,568	$329,318	$311,567	$1,295,668
51	$0	$0	$364,524	$422,694	$443,414	$346,480	$332,279	$1,295,668
52	$0	$0	$378,893	$452,283	$478,887	$364,673	$354,022	$1,295,668
53	$0	$0	$393,829	$483,943	$517,198	$384,012	$376,912	$1,295,668
54	$0	$0	$409,354	$517,819	$558,574	$409,493	$405,943	$1,295,668
55	$0	$0	$425,490	$554,066	$603,259	$441,357	$441,357	$1,295,668
56	$0	$0	$442,263	$592,850	$651,520	$475,804	$475,804	$1,295,668
57	$0	$0	$459,697	$634,350	$703,642	$513,050	$513,050	$1,295,668
58	$0	$0	$477,819	$678,754	$759,933	$553,608	$553,608	$1,295,668
59	$0	$0	$496,654	$726,267	$820,728	$597,778	$597,778	$1,295,668
60	$0	$0	$516,232	$777,106	$886,386	$645,689	$645,689	$1,295,668
61	$0	$0	$536,582	$831,503	$957,297	$697,823	$697,823	$1,295,668
62	$0	$0	$557,734	$889,709	$1,033,881	$754,651	$754,651	$1,295,668
63	$0	$0	$579,720	$951,988	$1,116,591	$816,703	$816,703	$1,295,668
64	$0	$0	$602,573	$1,018,627	$1,205,918	$884,690	$884,690	$1,295,668
65	$0	$-70,547	$552,998	$975,194	$1,186,582	$882,180	$882,180	$1,225,096
66	$0	$-70,547	$501,469	$928,720	$1,165,698	$879,922	$879,922	$1,154,524

Where to Put the Extra Money - 167

67	$0	$-70,547	$447,909	$878,992	$1,143,144	$878,100	$878,100	$1,083,952
68	$0	$-70,547	$392,238	$825,784	$1,118,786	$876,934	$876,934	$1,026,013
69	$0	$-70,547	$334,372	$768,851	$1,092,479	$932,836	$876,276	$1,025,530
70	$0	$-70,547	$274,225	$707,933	$1,064,067	$1,010,997	$874,993	$1,026,642
71	$0	$-70,547	$211,707	$642,751	$1,033,383	$1,094,529	$873,519	$1,015,807
72	$0	$-70,547	$146,725	$573,006	$1,000,243	$1,183,869	$871,902	$1,002,128
73	$0	$-70,547	$79,180	$498,379	$964,453	$1,279,523	$870,234	$985,391
74	$0	$-70,547	$8,974	$418,528	$925,799	$1,382,072	$868,647	$965,392
75	$0	$-70,547	$0	$333,087	$884,053	$1,492,197	$867,348	$941,957
76	$0	$-70,547	$0	$241,665	$838,967	$1,609,597	$865,522	$946,002
77	$0	$-70,547	$0	$143,844	$790,275	$1,734,668	$863,023	$949,757
78	$0	$-70,547	$0	$39,176	$737,687	$1,867,839	$859,694	$953,086
79	$0	$-70,547	$0	$0	$680,892	$2,009,539	$855,338	$955,815
80	$0	$-70,547	$0	$0	$619,553	$2,160,229	$849,749	$957,760
81	$0	$-70,547	$0	$0	$553,307	$2,320,380	$842,681	$958,700
82	$0	$-70,547	$0	$0	$481,762	$2,490,516	$833,892	$958,418
83	$0	$-70,547	$0	$0	$404,493	$2,671,157	$823,085	$956,643
84	$0	$-70,547	$0	$0	$321,042	$2,862,724	$809,801	$952,937
85	$0	$-70,547	$0	$0	$230,916	$3,065,590	$793,477	$946,757
86	$0	$-70,547	$0	$0	$133,579	$3,280,031	$773,385	$937,386
87	$0	$-70,547	$0	$0	$28,456	$3,506,446	$748,850	$924,172
88	$0	$-70,547	$0	$0	$0	$3,745,302	$719,189	$906,454
89	$0	$-70,547	$0	$0	$0	$3,997,120	$683,693	$883,549
90	$0	$-70,547	$0	$0	$0	$4,262,375	$641,523	$854,641
91	$0	$-70,547	$0	$0	$0	$4,547,298	$597,501	$779,393
92	$0	$-70,547	$0	$0	$0	$4,854,492	$552,724	$698,359
93	$0	$-70,547	$0	$0	$0	$5,186,992	$508,615	$612,355
94	$0	$-70,547	$0	$0	$0	$5,549,012	$467,663	$523,153
95	$0	$-70,547	$0	$0	$0	$5,934,141	$421,612	$480,954
96	$0	$-70,547	$0	$0	$0	$6,343,897	$370,006	$433,445
97	$0	$-70,547	$0	$0	$0	$6,780,159	$312,611	$380,412
98	$0	$-70,547	$0	$0	$0	$7,244,446	$248,684	$321,128

(*Figure 7.3* ~ This illustrates the non-guaranteed values for all years. Actual results will be lower or higher.)

The total funds committed to this comparison were $300,000 over a 5 year period. The Amount withdrawn from the Indexed Universal Life over 33 years is $2,398,598 with $248,684 still left in the policy at age 98. The CD ran out of money at age 75, the annuity at age 79 and the IRA at age 88.

168 - The New Mortgage Investment Advisor

This illustration is based on the same 45 year old male withdrawing $300,000 of equity for supplemental retirement income. However, this time we are electing the variable loan option for the withdrawal phase.

	Tax Type	Interest Rate	Management Fee	Premature Dist. Tax	Sales Charge
Certificate of Deposit	Taxable	6.00%	0.00%	0.00%	0.00%
Annuity	Deferred	7.00%	0.00%	10.00%	0.00%
IRA/401(k)	Deferred	9.00%	1.00%	10.00%	0.00%
Indexed Universal Life Insurance	Tax Advantaged	8.00%			

Withdrawals are Done with the Variable Loan Option at 1% Arbitrage.

Age	Contribution (Premium)	After Tax Amount of Withdrawal (Loan)	After Tax Values — Certificate of Deposit	After Tax Values — Annuity	After Tax Values — IRA	Insurance Values — Cash Value	Insurance Values — Surrender Value	Insurance Values — Death Benefit
45	$60,000	$0	$62,365	$64,200	$64,800	$53,758	$31,978	$1,295,668
46	$60,000	$0	$127,189	$132,894	$134,784	$111,562	$79,624	$1,295,668
47	$60,000	$0	$194,568	$206,397	$210,367	$173,800	$145,411	$1,295,668
48	$60,000	$0	$264,603	$285,044	$291,996	$240,855	$216,018	$1,295,668
49	$60,000	$0	$337,399	$369,197	$380,156	$313,111	$291,823	$1,295,668
50	$0	$0	$350,699	$395,041	$410,568	$329,318	$311,567	$1,295,668
51	$0	$0	$364,524	$422,694	$443,414	$346,480	$332,279	$1,295,668
52	$0	$0	$378,893	$452,283	$478,887	$364,673	$354,022	$1,295,668
53	$0	$0	$393,829	$483,943	$517,198	$384,012	$376,912	$1,295,668
54	$0	$0	$409,354	$517,819	$558,574	$409,493	$405,943	$1,295,668
55	$0	$0	$425,490	$554,066	$603,259	$441,357	$441,357	$1,295,668
56	$0	$0	$442,263	$592,850	$651,520	$475,804	$475,804	$1,295,668
57	$0	$0	$459,697	$634,350	$703,642	$513,050	$513,050	$1,295,668
58	$0	$0	$477,819	$678,754	$759,933	$553,608	$553,608	$1,295,668
59	$0	$0	$496,654	$726,267	$820,728	$597,778	$597,778	$1,295,668
60	$0	$0	$516,232	$777,106	$886,386	$645,689	$645,689	$1,295,668
61	$0	$0	$536,582	$831,503	$957,297	$697,823	$697,823	$1,295,668
62	$0	$0	$557,734	$889,709	$1,033,881	$754,651	$754,651	$1,295,668
63	$0	$0	$579,720	$951,988	$1,116,591	$816,703	$816,703	$1,295,668
64	$0	$0	$602,573	$1,018,627	$1,205,918	$884,690	$884,690	$1,295,668
65	$0	$-106,607	$515,517	$916,546	$1,127,386	$959,349	$845,279	$1,181,599
66	$0	$-106,607	$425,029	$807,318	$1,042,571	$1,041,570	$805,446	$1,059,544
67	$0	$-106,607	$330,974	$690,445	$950,970	$1,132,321	$765,599	$969,417
68	$0	$-106,607	$233,212	$565,390	$852,042	$1,231,673	$725,211	$934,595
69	$0	$-106,607	$131,595	$431,582	$745,199	$1,339,974	$683,990	$898,386
70	$0	$-106,607	$25,973	$288,407	$629,809	$1,457,462	$641,490	$860,109
71	$0	$-106,607	$0	$135,210	$505,187	$1,585,756	$598,597	$804,745
72	$0	$-106,607	$0	$0	$370,596	$1,725,956	$555,626	$745,481
73	$0	$-106,607	$0	$0	$225,238	$1,879,320	$512,997	$682,135
74	$0	$-106,607	$0	$0	$68,251	$2,047,278	$471,243	$614,552
75	$0	$-106,607	$0	$0	$0	$2,231,493	$431,066	$542,640
76	$0	$-106,607	$0	$0	$0	$2,432,188	$391,662	$513,271

Where to Put the Extra Money - 169

77	$0	$-106,607	$0	$0	$0	$2,650,727	$353,294	$485,830
78	$0	$-106,607	$0	$0	$0	$2,888,595	$316,273	$460,703
79	$0	$-106,607	$0	$0	$0	$3,147,380	$280,925	$438,294
80	$0	$-106,607	$0	$0	$0	$3,428,807	$247,631	$419,072
81	$0	$-106,607	$0	$0	$0	$3,734,728	$216,800	$403,537
82	$0	$-106,607	$0	$0	$0	$4,067,197	$188,945	$392,305
83	$0	$-106,607	$0	$0	$0	$4,428,387	$164,588	$386,007
84	$0	$-106,607	$0	$0	$0	$4,820,442	$144,107	$385,129
85	$0	$-106,607	$0	$0	$0	$5,245,559	$127,811	$390,089
86	$0	$-106,607	$0	$0	$0	$5,705,911	$115,851	$401,147
87	$0	$-106,607	$0	$0	$0	$6,204,046	$108,612	$418,815
88	$0	$-106,607	$0	$0	$0	$6,742,805	$106,622	$443,762
89	$0	$-106,607	$0	$0	$0	$7,325,330	$110,544	$476,811
90	$0	$-106,607	$0	$0	$0	$7,954,901	$121,011	$518,756
91	$0	$-106,607	$0	$0	$0	$8,646,144	$149,812	$495,658
92	$0	$-106,607	$0	$0	$0	$9,407,404	$202,260	$484,482
93	$0	$-106,607	$0	$0	$0	$10,248,414	$284,840	$489,808
94	$0	$-106,607	$0	$0	$0	$11,181,907	$406,813	$518,632
95	$0	$-106,607	$0	$0	$0	$12,199,221	$555,801	$677,793
96	$0	$-106,607	$0	$0	$0	$13,308,061	$735,533	$868,613
97	$0	$-106,607	$0	$0	$0	$14,517,448	$950,773	$1,095,947
98	$0	$-106,607	$0	$0	$0	$15,836,162	$1,205,751	$1,364,112

(*Figure 7.4* ~ This illustrates the non-guaranteed values for all years. Actual results will be lower or higher.)

The total funds committed to this comparison were $300,000 over a 5 year period. The Amount withdrawn from the Indexed Universal Life over 33 years is $3,814,664 with $1,205,751 still left in the policy at age 98. The CD ran out of money at age 71, the annuity at age 72 and the IRA at age 75.

Equity Wealth Seminar Tickets

If you've gotten to this point, you have read through the book, understood the basic outline of the wealth generation strategies presented, and are most likely interested in what you have read. The most common question asked at this point is simply, "What now?"

If this book was given to you by a financial professional, then the first step is to contact the person who provided you a copy of this book.

The second step, for those interested in taking a more in depth, yet practical look at the strategies presented, we invite you to come to one of our Equity Wealth Seminars. The seminars are approximately 2 hours in length and educational in nature. No selling takes place at the seminars. Rather, the seminars are designed to extrapolate on the strategies you've become familiar with in the book. Further, after expanding on the strategies, time is spent in demonstrating how to implement and apply the strategies so you can begin your own process of generating wealth.

Our Equity Wealth Seminars are being presented constantly throughout the country, so check our website for dates and availability. Further, while the cost of the seminar is usually $149 per person/$248 per couple, there is a discount code listed at the bottom of this page that will provide free admittance to an Equity Wealth Seminar when registering via the internet at www.CMIADesignation.com or by calling Capital Republic Financial Group, Inc. at (800) 990-2734 or (714) 657-3559.

> Discount Code: 581FF

Appendix I
CMIA Designation

Attention Investment Professionals!!!
Financial Planners, Home Mortgage Planners, and Insurance Professionals

Some of the difficulty facing our industry is that with the increasing complexity of the tax code and the multitude of financial products on the market, it is difficult to keep abreast of all the new products, strategies, and information inundating our industry. Further, several of the strategies outlined in the book are quite sophisticated and require a solid working knowledge of mortgage loans, life insurance, financial planning, and, perhaps most significantly, how they all tie together.

To address both the issues of professional distinction and financial planning sophistication, the authors have designed a new course of study for professionals in our industry to earn the designation of Certified Mortgage Investment Advisor (CMIA). This designation will distinguish you as a financial professional with core knowledge of how life insurance can be utilized in retirement planning to leverage equity, grow investments tax deferred, to allow tax advantaged withdrawals of investments, and to minimize tax liability on inheritances, just to name a few.

The course requirements are rigorous and the course of study relevant and in line with the highest standards and practices of professionals in our industry. Candidates will complete a course of study culminating in a comprehensive exam. Upon completion of the course of study and successfully passing the course exam, you will be conferred the designation of CMIA.

For more information or to enroll in the Certified Mortgage Investment Advisor course, please inquire by calling Capital Republic Financial Group, Inc. at (800) 990-2734 or (714) 657-3559 or learn more now by visiting our website at www.CMIADesignation.com.

Appendix II
Glossary of Mortgage Terms

Glossary of Mortgage Terms

203(b): FHA program which provides mortgage insurance to protect lenders from default; used to finance the purchase of new or existing one- to four family housing; characterized by low down payment, flexible qualifying guidelines, limited fees, and a limit on maximum loan amount.

203(k): this FHA mortgage insurance program enables homebuyers to finance both the purchase of a house and the cost of its rehabilitation through a single mortgage loan.

A

Amenity: a feature of the home or property that serves as a benefit to the buyer but that is not necessary to its use; may be natural (like location, Woods, water) or man-made (like a swimming pool or garden).

Amortization: repayment of a mortgage loan through monthly installments of principal and interest; the monthly payment amount is based on a schedule that will allow you to own your home at the end of a specific time period (for example, 15 or 30 years).

Annual Percentage Rate (APR): calculated by using a standard formula, the APR shows the cost of a loan; expressed as a yearly interest rate, it includes the interest, points, mortgage insurance, and other fees associated with the loan.

Application: the first step in the official loan approval process; this form is used to record important information about the potential borrower necessary to the underwriting process.

Appraisal: a document that gives an estimate of a property's fair market value; an appraisal is generally required by a lender before loan approval to ensure that the mortgage loan amount is not more than the value of the property.

Appraiser: a qualified individual who uses his or her experience and knowledge to prepare the appraisal estimate.

Arbitrage: a kind of hedged investment meant to capture slight differences in price; when there is a difference in the price of something on two different markets the arbitrageur simultaneously buys at the lower price and sells at the higher price.

ARM: Adjustable Rate Mortgage; a mortgage loan subject to changes in interest rates; when rates change, ARM monthly payments increase or decrease at intervals determined by the lender; the Change in monthly - payment amount, however, is usually subject to a Cap.

Assessor: a government official who is responsible for determining the value of a property for the purpose of taxation.

Assumable mortgage: a mortgage that can be transferred from a seller to a buyer; once the loan is assumed by the buyer the seller is no longer responsible for repaying it; there may be a fee and/or a credit package involved in the transfer of an assumable mortgage.

B

Balloon Mortgage: a mortgage that typically offers low rates for an initial period of time (usually 5, 7, or 10) years; after that time period elapses, the balance is due or is refinanced by the borrower.

Bankruptcy: a federal law whereby a person's assets are turned over to a trustee and used to pay off outstanding debts; this usually occurs when someone owes more than they have the ability to repay.

Borrower: a person who has been approved to receive a loan and is then obligated to repay it and any additional fees according to the loan terms.

Building code: based on agreed upon safety standards within a specific area, a building code is a regulation that determines the design, construction, and materials used in building.

Budget: a detailed record of all income earned and spent during a specific period of time.

C

Cap: a limit, such as that placed on an adjustable rate mortgage, on how much a monthly payment or interest rate can increase or decrease.

Cash reserves: a cash amount sometimes required to be held in reserve in addition to the down payment and closing costs; the amount is determined by the lender.

Certificate of title: a document provided by a qualified source (such as a title company) that shows the property legally belongs to the current owner; before the title is transferred at closing, it should be clear and free of all liens or other claims.

Closing: also known as settlement, this is the time at which the property is formally sold and transferred from the seller to the buyer; it is at this time that the borrower takes on the loan obligation, pays all closing costs, and receives title from the seller.

Closing costs: customary costs above and beyond the sale price of the property that must be paid to cover the transfer of ownership at closing; these costs generally vary by geographic location and are typically detailed to the borrower after submission of a loan application.

Commission: an amount, usually a percentage of the property sales price that is collected by a real estate professional as a fee for negotiating the transaction.

Condominium: a form of ownership in which individuals purchase and own a unit of housing in a multi-unit complex; the owner also shares financial responsibility for common areas.

Conventional loan: a private sector loan, one that is not guaranteed or insured by the U.S. government.

Cooperative (Co-op): residents purchase stock in a cooperative corporation that owns a structure; each stockholder is then entitled to live in a specific unit of the structure and is responsible for paying a portion of the loan.

Credit history: history of an individual's debt payment; lenders use this information to gauge a potential borrower's ability to repay a loan.

Credit report: a record that lists all past and present debts and the timeliness of their repayment; it documents an individual's credit history.

Credit bureau score: a number representing the possibility a borrower may default; it is based upon credit history and is used to determine ability to qualify for a mortgage loan.

D

Debt-to-income ratio: a comparison of gross income to housing and non-housing expenses; With the FHA, the-monthly mortgage payment should be no more than 29% of monthly gross income (before taxes) and the mortgage payment combined with non-housing debts should not exceed 41% of income.

Deed: the document that transfers ownership of a property.

Deed-in-lieu: to avoid foreclosure ("in lieu" of foreclosure), a deed is given to the lender to fulfill the obligation to repay the debt; this process doesn't allow the borrower to remain in the house but helps avoid the costs, time, and effort associated with foreclosure.

Default: the inability to pay monthly mortgage payments in a timely manner or to otherwise meet the mortgage terms.

Delinquency: failure of a borrower to make timely mortgage payments under a loan agreement.

Discount point: normally paid at closing and generally calculated to be equivalent to 1% of the total loan amount, discount points are paid to reduce the interest rate on a loan.

Down payment: the portion of a home's purchase price that is paid in cash and is not part of the mortgage loan.

E

Earnest money: money put down by a potential buyer to show that he or she is serious about purchasing the home; it becomes part of the down payment if the offer is accepted, is returned if the offer is rejected, or is forfeited if the buyer pulls out of the deal.

EEM: Energy Efficient Mortgage; an FHA program that helps homebuyers save money on utility bills by enabling them to finance the cost of adding energy efficiency features to a new or existing home as part of the home purchase

Equity: an owner's financial interest in a property; calculated by subtracting the amount still owed on the mortgage loon(s)from the fair market value of the property.

Escrow account: a separate account into which the lender puts a portion of each monthly mortgage payment; an escrow account provides the funds needed for such expenses as property taxes, homeowners insurance, mortgage insurance, etc.

F

Fair Housing Act: a law that prohibits discrimination in all facets of the home buying process on the basis of race, color, national origin, religion, sex, familial status, or disability.

Fair market value: the hypothetical price that a willing buyer and seller will agree upon when they are acting freely, carefully, and with complete knowledge of the situation.

Fannie Mae: Federal National Mortgage Association (FNMA); a federally-chartered enterprise owned by private stockholders that purchases residential mortgages and converts them into securities for sale to investors; by purchasing mortgages, Fannie Mae supplies funds that lenders may loan to potential homebuyers.

FHA: Federal Housing Administration; established in 1934 to advance homeownership opportunities for all Americans; assists homebuyers by providing mortgage insurance to lenders to cover most losses that may occur when a borrower defaults; this encourages lenders to make loans to borrowers who might not qualify for conventional mortgages.

Fixed-rate mortgage: a mortgage with payments that remain the same throughout the life of the loan because the interest rate and other terms are fixed and do not change.

Flood insurance: insurance that protects homeowners against losses from a flood; if a home is located in a flood plain; the lender will require flood insurance before approving a loan.

Foreclosure: a legal process in which mortgaged property is sold to pay the loan of the defaulting borrower.

Freddie Mac: Federal Home Loan Mortgage Corporation (FHLM); a federally-chartered corporation that purchases residential mortgages, securitizes them, and sells them to investors; this provides lenders with funds for new homebuyers.

G

Ginnie Mae: Government National Mortgage Association (GNMA); a government-owned corporation overseen by the U.S. Department of Housing and Urban Development, Ginnie Mae pools FHA-insured and VA-guaranteed loans to back securities for private investment; as With Fannie Mae and Freddie Mac, the investment income provides funding that may then be lent to eligible borrowers by lenders.

Good faith estimate: an estimate of all closing fees including pre-paid and escrow items as well as lender charges; must be given to the borrower within three days after submission of a loan application.

H

HELP: Homebuyer Education Learning Program; an educational program from the FHA that counsels people about the home buying process; HELP covers topics like budgeting, finding a home, getting a loan, and home maintenance; in most cases, completion of the program may entitle the homebuyer to a reduced initial FHA mortgage insurance premium-from 2.25% to 1.75% of the home purchase price.

Home inspection: an examination of the structure and mechanical systems to determine a home's safety; makes the potential homebuyer aware of any repairs that may be needed.

Home warranty: offers protection for mechanical systems and attached appliances against unexpected repairs not covered by homeowner's insurance. Coverage extends over a specific time period and does not cover the home's structure.

Homeowner's insurance: an insurance policy that combines protection against damage to a dwelling and its contents with protection against claims of negligence or inappropriate action that result in someone's injury or property damage.

Housing counseling agency- provides counseling and assistance to individuals on a variety of issues, including loan default, fair housing, and home buying.

HUD: the U.S. Department of Housing and Urban Development; established in 1965, HUD works to create a decent home and suitable living environment for all Americans; it does this by addressing housing needs, improving and developing American communities, and enforcing fair housing laws.

HUD1 Statement: also known as the "settlement sheet," it itemizes all closing costs; must be given to the borrower at or before closing.

HVAC: Heating, Ventilation and Air Conditioning; a home's heating and cooling system.

I

Index. a measurement used by lenders to determine changes to the Interest rate charged on an adjustable rate mortgage.

Inflation: the number of dollars in circulation exceeds the amount of goods and services available for purchase; inflation results in a decrease in the dollar's value.

Interest: a fee charged for the use of money.

Interest rate: the amount of interest charged on a monthly loan payment; usually expressed as a percentage.

Insurance: protection against a specific loss over a period of time that is secured by the payment of a regularly scheduled premium.

J

Judgment: a legal decision; when requiring debt repayment, a judgment may include a property lien that secures the creditor's claim by providing a collateral source.

L

Lease purchase: assists low- to moderate-income homebuyers in purchasing a home by allowing them to lease a home with an option to buy; the rent payment is made up of the monthly rental payment plus an additional amount that is credited to an account for use as a down payment.

Lien: a legal claim against property that must be satisfied When the property is sold

Loan: money borrowed that is usually repaid with interest.

Loan fraud: purposely giving incorrect information on a loan application in order to better qualify for a loan; may result in civil liability or criminal penalties.

Loan-to-value (LTV) ratio.- a percentage calculated by dividing the amount borrowed by the price or appraised value of the home to be purchased; the higher the LTV, the less cash a borrower is required to pay as down payment.

Lock-in: since interest rates can change frequently, many lenders offer an interest rate lock-in that guarantees a specific interest rate if the loan is closed within a specific time.

Loss mitigation: a process to avoid foreclosure; the lender tries to help a borrower who has been unable to make loan payments and is in danger of defaulting on his or her loan

M

Margin: an amount the lender adds to an index to determine the interest rate on an adjustable rate mortgage.

Mortgage: a lien on the property that secures the Promise to repay a loan.

Mortgage banker: a company that originates loans and resells them to secondary mortgage lenders like: Fannie Mae or Freddie Mac.

Mortgage broker: a firm that originates and processes loans for a number of lenders.

Mortgage insurance: a policy that protects lenders against some or most of the losses that can occur when a borrower defaults on a mortgage loan; mortgage insurance is required primarily for borrowers with a down payment of less than 20% of the home's purchase price.

Mortgage insurance premium (MIP): a monthly payment -usually part of the mortgage payment - paid by a borrower for mortgage insurance.

Mortgage Modification: a loss mitigation option that allows a borrower to refinance and/or extend the term of the mortgage loan and thus reduce the monthly payments.

O

Offer: indication by a potential buyer of a willingness to purchase a home at a specific price; generally put forth in writing.

Origination: the process of preparing, submitting, and evaluating a loan application; generally includes a credit check, verification of employment, and a property appraisal.

Origination fee: the charge for originating a loan; is usually calculated in the form of points and paid at closing.

P

Partial Claim: a loss mitigation option offered by the FHA that allows a borrower, with help from a lender, to get an interest-free loan from HUD to bring their mortgage payments up to date.

PITI: Principal, Interest, Taxes, and Insurance - the four elements of a monthly mortgage payment; payments of principal and interest go directly towards repaying the loan while the portion that covers taxes and insurance (homeowner's and mortgage, if applicable) goes into an escrow account to cover the fees when they are due.

PMI: Private Mortgage Insurance; privately-owned companies that offer standard and special affordable mortgage insurance programs for qualified borrowers with down payments of less than 20% of a purchase price.

Pre-approve: lender commits to lend to a potential borrower; commitment remains as long as the borrower still meets the qualification requirements at the time of purchase.

Pre-foreclosure sale: allows a defaulting borrower to sell the mortgaged property to satisfy the loan and avoid foreclosure.

Appendix II- Glossary of Mortgage Terms - 189

Pre-qualify: a lender informally determines the maximum amount an individual is eligible to borrow.

Premium: an amount paid on a regular schedule by a policyholder that maintains insurance coverage.

Prepayment: payment of the mortgage loan before the scheduled due date; may be Subject to a prepayment penalty.

PrincipalT: the amount borrowed from a lender; doesn't include interest or additional fees.

R

Radon: a radioactive gas found in some homes that, if occurring in strong enough concentrations, can cause health problems.

Real estate agent: an individual who is licensed to negotiate and arrange real estate sales; works for a real estate broker.

REALTOR: a real estate agent or broker who is a member of the NATIONAL ASSOCIATION OF REALTORS, and its local and state associations.

Refinancing: paying off one loan by obtaining another; refinancing is generally done to secure better loan terms (like a lower interest rate).

Rehabilitation mortgage: a mortgage that covers the costs of rehabilitating (repairing or Improving) a property; some rehabilitation mortgages - like the FHA's 203(k) - allow a borrower to roll the costs of rehabilitation and home purchase into one mortgage loan.

RESPA: Real Estate Settlement Procedures Act; a law protecting consumers from abuses during the residential real estate purchase and loan process by requiring lenders to disclose all settlement costs, practices, and relationships

S

Settlement: another name for closing.

Special Forbearance: a loss mitigation option where the lender arranges a revised repayment plan for the borrower that may include a temporary reduction or suspension of monthly loan payments.

Subordinate: to place in a rank of lesser importance or to make one claim secondary to another.

Survey: a property diagram that indicates legal boundaries, easements, encroachments, rights of way, improvement locations, etc.

Sweat equity: using labor to build or improve a property as part of the down payment

T

Title 1: an FHA-insured loan that allows a borrower to make non-luxury improvements (like renovations or repairs) to their home; Title I loans less than $7,500 don't require a property lien.

Title insurance: insurance that protects the lender against any claims that arise from arguments about ownership of the property; also available for homebuyers.

Title search: a check of public records to be sure that the seller is the recognized owner of the real estate and that there are no unsettled liens or other claims against the property.

Truth-in-Lending: a federal law obligating a lender to give full written disclosure of all fees, terms, and conditions associated with the loan initial period and then adjusts to another rate that lasts for the term of the loan.

U

Underwriting: the process of analyzing a loan application to determine the amount of risk involved in making the loan; it includes a review of the potential borrower's credit history and a judgment of the property value.

V

VA: Department of Veterans Affairs: a federal agency which guarantees loans made to veterans; similar to mortgage insurance, a loan guarantee protects lenders against loss that may result from a borrower default.

About Peter D. Mitchell

Pete Mitchell has been in the financial planning/insurance industry for over a decade. He is currently the Chief Investment Officer and President of Capital Republic Financial Group, Inc. In addition to a B.A. from Biola University, Pete holds the designations of Accredited Asset Management Specialist (AAMS) earned through The College for Financial Planning in Greenwood, Colorado. Additionally, he is a Certified Fee Insurance Specialist (CFIS) and on the board of directors for Apologetics.com, Inc, a non-profit organization.

About James D. Pidd, II

Jim Pidd earned his B.A. and M.A. from Biola University. As an educator Jim has taught across the educational spectrum from elementary school to graduate school. He is a successful real estate investor with an involvement in both commercial and residential real estate in several states across the nation. He currently resides in Lakewood, CA with his wife Karen and their two children Timothy and Gwendolyn.

To contact the authors, email
info@newmortgageinvestmentadvisor.com